ABOUT THE AUTHOR

Jonathan Hobbs graduated in Finance and Economics from the University of Cape Town, South Africa in 2006. Since then he has kept himself busy working in London for various financial firms such as Morgan Stanley, HSBC and M&G Investments. He holds the Chartered Financial Analyst ® Designation.

In June 2017, Jonathan left his work in the city to focus his efforts full time as an entrepreneur, author and investor. During that year, he started the www.stopsaving.com investor blog, which covers a wide range of investment-related topics. In his personal portfolio, he invests in stocks, mutual funds, startup companies, gold and now cryptocurrencies.

Jonathan believes strongly that nobody can predict the future of financial markets. For this reason, he simplifies his approach to investing with basic investment rules and strategies that work well over time.

THE CRYPTO PORTFOLIO

A COMMONSENSE APPROACH TO CRYPTOCURRENCY INVESTING

JONATHAN HOBBS, CFA

Disclaimer: The information and advice presented in this book are for educational purposes. Any examples used are for educational and illustrative purposes only. Neither the author nor any companies owned by the author are regulated by the Financial Conduct Authority (FCA) nor any other financial regulator. This book is not recommending investments in cryptocurrencies, stocks, mutual funds, investments or securities of any kind.

Neither the author, the publisher nor the companies owned by the author shall have any liability to any person or entity with respect to any loss or damage caused by or alleged to be caused directly or indirectly by the instruction contained in this book or by the computer software or websites described in it. Past performance and any examples or testimonials cited are no indication or guarantee of anticipated future results. Individual results will vary and cannot be guaranteed.

ISBN: 9781973553922
Website: www.stopsaving.com

For my mom, who showed me how to help others,
and for my dad, who gave me a copy of Napoleon Hill's book, *Think and Grow Rich*, before I was old enough to understand it.

CONTENTS

INTRODUCTION

This is a book about investing in cryptocurrencies (or *cryptos* if you're street). If you are currently asking yourself questions like:

- What are cryptos?
- Should I invest in cryptos?
- How do I invest in cryptos in a sensible way without taking too much risk?

...then I hope this book answers your questions. I am not making any predictions on whether the cryptocurrency market will go up or down in the near future - there's enough of that in the media already. Instead, I explain how cryptos work and explore some of the ways to potentially lower the risks of investing in them. I try to do this in a language that people without financial or computer science backgrounds can easily understand.

This book is split into three parts:

1. In part one, we explore what cryptos are, and why the technology behind them - blockchain - is taking the world by storm. We look under the hood at how cryptocurrencies like Bitcoin, Ripple, Dash, Litecoin, and Monero use blockchain for secure financial transactions. Next, we focus on Ethereum, and how its smart contracts and decentralized applications are changing everything from complex financial derivatives to election voting. We then move on to crypto *forks*, before going over an interesting cryptocurrency called IOTA, which doesn't use blockchain at all. Other newer and exciting cryptos like Neo, Cardano and Stratis are briefly discussed along the way.

2. Part two covers an automated strategy for investing in cryptos in a simple and sensible way. Because we don't know what the future holds, the *Crypto Portfolio (CP)* strategy is designed to help reduce the risks of crypto investing, of which there are many! You'll also learn about crypto exchanges and wallet storage methods, what to do about crypto taxes, how to monitor the performance of your Crypto Portfolio and more. The CP Strategy is

designed so that you only invest once a month. It's a *leave and forget* investment strategy that is not meant to take up a lot of your time.

3. Part three covers more advanced crypto trading and investing strategies. These include fundamental coin analysis, initial coin offerings (ICOs) and the dark arts of technical analysis. These chapters will serve you well if you are looking to take a more active approach to crypto investing than what is covered in the CP strategy of part two. The strategies discussed in part three are skills based, meaning they take time to master. Part three, therefore, serves as a foundational course for active crypto investing, which will give you enough information to decide on your next steps.

I hope you enjoy reading this book, and that you walk away with some tools and insight to help you navigate investing in this new, exciting and rapidly evolving asset class.

To your investment success,

Jonathan Hobbs, CFA

SOME IMPORTANT POINTS BEFORE WE BEGIN

To get the most out of this book, it's worth keeping the below twenty points at the back of your mind. Some of these apply to investing in general, not just cryptocurrency investing.

1. In this book, cryptos, coins and cryptocurrencies all mean the same thing. As you'll learn in the chapters to follow, there are many different types of coins, which have various different purposes.

2. The prices of bitcoin and other cryptocurrencies have already gone up thousands of times, making some people rich very quickly. Just because they got rich by investing in cryptos, doesn't mean you will too. Nobody really knows whether prices will keep going up for years to come, or crash by 90% tomorrow and never reach new highs. It's hard enough trying to predict the future of any financial market, let alone cryptos, which are a brand-new type of investment.

3. Stories about massive investment opportunities or impending financial doom both make for better media headlines than the boring stuff in between. Half the experts in the media will tell you to buy and hold bitcoin and other cryptos because they're going to the *moon*. The other half will tell you cryptos are in the biggest bubble of all time, which could burst any day now. Pay them no attention. Do your own research and empower yourself to make your own investment decisions. You are responsible for your financial future, not the media.

4. Regardless of your belief about the future of cryptos right now, you owe it to yourself to read this book so you can at least understand what they are about. You should never invest in anything you don't understand, so take time getting to grips with the content from part one of this book before moving on to the investing sections in parts two and three.

5. Crypto prices often drop 15% in a day and sometimes by much more. So, if you are going to invest in cryptos, do it with a strategy that makes the process less risky. You can only lose the money you invest, so don't invest a lot. Conversely, crypto returns can also be very high at times, so you shouldn't need to invest a lot of money to potentially see positive effects to your finances over time.

6. There are many different opinions as to which coin will dominate the crypto market in a few years' time. Trying to pick a single winner now will most likely doom you from the start. Diversify instead by investing in a basket of different coins.

7. Don't just diversify your crypto investments, diversify *all* your investments. Own a spread of different types of assets. Stocks, bonds, mutual funds, ETFs, gold, silver, property, fine art, wine, timber, personal businesses, angel startup investments. There are lots to choose from. Pick at least three and learn how to invest in them effectively. If you're still unsure which assets you want to invest in, learn about them all and then decide. Different investments build wealth over time, but they don't all go up at the same time.

8. No matter how many books you read, there are no substitutes for *learning by doing*. Don't expect to make any money your first year of investing. I lost money in mine, but the lessons I learned that year have more than made up for it.

9. Investing is far less stressful when you follow a sound investment strategy, so spend time formulating your strategy before you invest.

10. It takes a long time to learn how to spend less time investing. The time you spend learning how to do this is the best investment you will ever make.

11. Don't ever borrow money to invest, unless it's something like buy-to-let property where your rental income covers your loan repayments. You'll be surprised how stress-free life can be without leverage.

12. When you get your paycheck each month, pay yourself first by investing at least ten percent of your hard-earned salary into your

investment portfolio. One day you'll wake up without any financial worries.

13. You won't get rich by saving money in your bank account. Over many years, investment returns exponentially compound upon themselves like a snowball rolling down a hill. Interest rates on savings barely keep up with inflation, if at all, so you are actually getting poorer each year by saving.

14. Some people think investing is riskier than saving. This isn't true. Investing isn't gambling if done properly. The biggest risk of saving is that you end up poor when you retire because your savings are worth less than they are now. Some years your investments will go up, some years they will go down. But in the end, you'll be far better off investing sensibly than you would be saving money in your bank account.

15. Treat your investment portfolio like a business. Build a spreadsheet with a graph plotting the returns of all your assets. Give your *multi-asset portfolio* a name that excites you. Then look at your portfolio now and again to see how you are doing. Once a year, do a deep dive to see how your business has performed. Try to do better next year.

16. Don't make emotional investment decisions. Logic is better.

17. If you lose 50% of your money, you need to make 100% to get back to where you started, so don't risk it. If you manage your risks, you have less chance of losing half your money in a year, and more chance of growing your money to a considerable sum over time.

18. At all costs, avoid FOMO (fear of missing out) when investing. There will always be other opportunities for the patient investor.

19. Financial freedom means being in a position where you don't have to work for money to pay your living expenses, however modest or lavish those may be. Instead, you can pursue your passions in life while your assets earn investment returns for you.

20. If you decide that you want to be financially free one day, you will. Having the right mindset will always be your best asset!

PART 1: WHAT ARE CRYPTOS?

CHAPTER 1

BLOCKCHAIN: WHAT'S ALL THE FUSS ABOUT?

"Blockchain is the tech. Bitcoin is merely the first mainstream manifestation of its potential"

Marc Kenigsberg

Blockchain is a big deal these days amongst investors, companies, technologists and this particular author. We'll cover the technical aspects of blockchain technology throughout part one of this book, but in this chapter, we first look at blockchain from the top level. Understanding the 'blockchain big picture' will lay the foundation for the chapters ahead.

Who invented blockchain?

Satoshi Nakamoto officially invented blockchain on October 31st, 2008[1], by emailing the **Bitcoin whitepaper** (the technical plan for how Bitcoin works) to a group of very clever and like-minded computer coders. As luck would have it, this was less than three weeks after the start of the 2008 financial crisis, when the Lehman Brothers investment bank collapsed.

The true identity of Satoshi Nakamoto is an unsolved mystery. But whomever Satoshi is, he (or she, they) has billions of dollars' worth of bitcoins and no desire to be famous!

What is blockchain?

Blockchain is the technology that makes bitcoin and other cryptocurrencies work. Without them we would not have cryptos, and you would not be reading this book. To explain the basics of blockchain, let's use the example of a simple financial transaction between two people...

The below illustration shows what happens if I send you money using my online bank account (without blockchain):

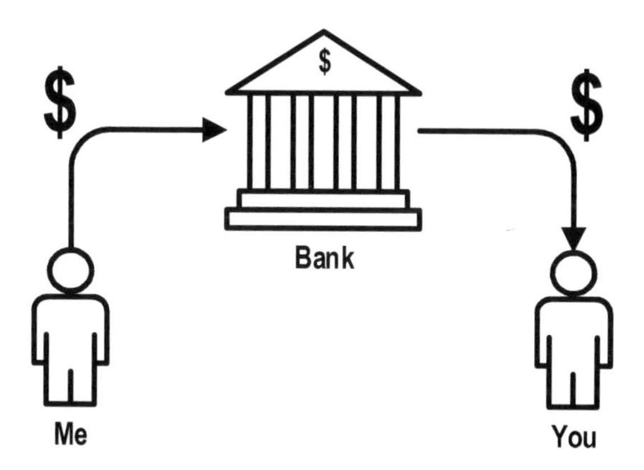

To keep things simple, assume we both use the same bank. In order to process the payment, the bank needs to debit my bank account and credit yours. The bank also looks after our money, making sure we always have easy access to it.

But what if there's a financial crisis and all the bank's customers want to withdraw their money at the same time? Since banks don't always keep everyone's money 'at the bank' (they lend most of it out), there's a chance we won't be able to access our funds. Or worse, what if the bank shuts down completely? This happened to the New York Bank of the United States in 1931, Northern Rock in 2008 and the Bank of Cyprus in 2011...to name a few.

Getting money *out* of a bank during a financial meltdown could be a problem. The next issue has to do with getting money *into* one. Today, there are over two billion people without a bank account[2]. They don't have access to basic financial services like saving and taking out a home mortgage. Most of them live in rural areas of third world countries, where there aren't many banks. But some live in developed countries like the UK and the USA and can't get a bank account because no bank will approve them.

Being unemployed can make it harder to open a bank account - and having no bank account can make it harder to find employment. It may be that the banks are just protecting themselves here, but that doesn't make things fair. Surely everyone should have access to their own bank account?

Apart from the potential issues of getting money in and out of them, there are also inefficiencies with banks and other financial middlemen. International money transfers are slow and have high fees - and the exchange rates aren't exactly 'spot price'. In 2018, sending money across the globe should be as fast and cheap as sending an email.

Then there are the security issues. Our financial data is stored in *one* place - our bank's online database - meaning a hacker has a single point from which to attack. If you call your bank, they usually ask you all kinds of security questions, so you can prove your identity. They do this for good reason, but the process can be frustrating at times. To protect you from being frauded, process your accounts, lend you money and use their services, banks must also store your personal information.

Enter Blockchain

Even if you have the best bank in the world, things can still go wrong. High fees, inefficiencies, security issues, trouble opening an account or withdrawing money in a crisis are all problems that can end with blockchain. Blockchain means we don't need to *trust* a bank - or any middleman for that matter - to always keep things safe, efficient and fair.

The diagram over the page shows what that transaction between you and I would look like without a bank in the middle...

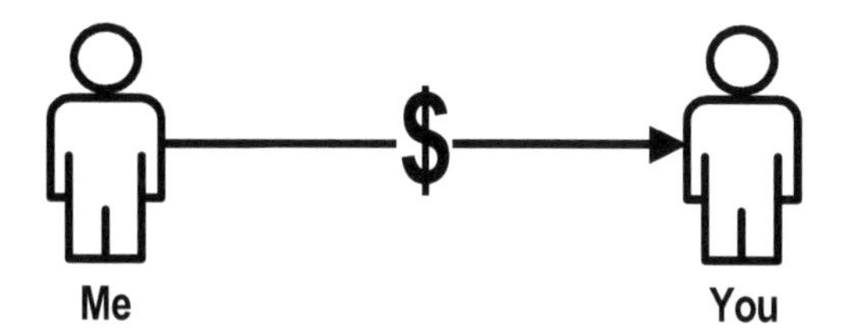

It's obviously a bit more complicated than this on the blockchain (we'll get there in the next chapter), but the simple illustration above shows why Satoshi created blockchain in the first place[1]: *to cut out the middleman.* This stops the potential security threats, high fees and inefficiencies that could be caused from having a middleman.

Imagine a global database of all the transactions that have ever happened. Everyone in the world can access it at the same time - either at a web address or by downloading a copy of it to their home computer or smartphone. Instead of showing the personal details of each transaction, the database shows *encrypted* addresses that can only be unlocked by their rightful owners.

Now imagine the global database never made a mistake, could never be hacked and always told the truth. Imagine that each transaction was verified by the consensus of every computer using the database, and to go against it would be to go against every one of those computers.

Definition of a blockchain

In its simplest form, a blockchain is a global network of computers all working together to confirm who owns what. The 'what' doesn't have to be in the form of financial value (like bitcoin) - it can also be information, digital rights or data of any kind.

The more computers using a blockchain, the stronger it becomes. Because blockchain is ***decentralized*** *(not controlled by one entity), there are no central points of weakness. This makes blockchain more*

[1] Satoshi Nakamoto explains this in more detail in the Bitcoin whitepaper, which you can read at https://bitcoin.org/bitcoin.pdf.

secure than the centralized databases of all banks, governments, Googles, Facebooks and Amazons.

Computers using blockchain are incentivized to do the right thing because they receive rewards (monetary or otherwise) for doing so. At the same time, they are discouraged from going against the blockchain because it would be a complete waste of time and resources to do that.

Further, blockchain uses ***secure cryptography*** *to make sure it can't be tampered with. This way, blockchain always tells the truth and, if needed, helps protect the privacy of the people using it.*

Blockchain doesn't just work for simple financial transactions. It can work for any online transfer of information or value.

With **smart contracts**, which we'll go over in chapter four, blockchain goes one step further. In the future, most legal contracts, insurance claims, financial derivatives, pension funds, crowdfunding raises and investment strategies will be programmed into smart contracts on some sort of blockchain. Be it a **private blockchain**, which can only be accessed by a few, or a **public blockchain**, which is open to the world.

What else could blockchains do?

Dropbox, Google Drive and iCloud are all great ways to store important information in the cloud. But all 'in the cloud' means here is that your information is stored within the online databases of those companies. Even though such databases use advanced security measures, they still have central points of potential failure.

With blockchain, no central authority, government or company would ever have the responsibility of looking after your personal data. This means your personal information would never be lost, hacked, or deleted. Things like identify fraud would be impossible, as would covert terrorist attacks made possible by hackers gaining access to important centralized databases.

Before the internet, most people were perfectly happy sending letters by postal mail, paying for stuff with checks and reading the newspaper. They then discovered they could send information and value 'through the air' via the internet. When the internet first started, we never understood how it worked. Most people still don't. But look at what the internet has allowed us to achieve.

Blockchain is the next step in the evolution of the internet - that's kind of a big deal. And just like when the internet first started some thirty odd years ago, we have no idea where it will take us.

Chapter Summary

1. *Satoshi Nakamoto, whose identity is unknown, officially invented blockchain in 2008 by publishing the Bitcoin whitepaper.*

2. *No matter how good your middleman is, it can make mistakes, charge high fees, store your data and is a single point of attack for fraudsters who want your money and personal information.*

3. *Blockchain doesn't need a middleman to make it work. That's the point.*

4. *Simple financial transactions are the first thing blockchain was used for. There are more uses today and there will be much more tomorrow.*

CHAPTER 2

BITCOIN: WHAT YOU NEED TO KNOW

"I've been working on a new electronic cash system that is fully peer-to-peer, with no trusted third party"

Satoshi Nakamoto

Bitcoin was the first blockchain based cryptocurrency. It was also the second most searched term in Google in the *Global News* category in 2017 - right behind Hurricane Irma[3]. On that note, I'm guessing you already know a bit about Bitcoin, so I hope this chapter adds to your knowledge in some way.

Bitcoin is two things:

1. A **digital form of money** that people can use to buy stuff with (bitcoin with a small 'b').

2. A **system** that supports the use of that digital money (Bitcoin with a big 'B').

Bitcoin as digital money

Digital money is a way to transfer value online. This can be through mobile phone apps, credit cards, PayPal, air miles, gift vouchers, supermarket reward points, online money transfers and so on. With digital money, we don't need to carry cash around in order to buy stuff; we can buy most things online from anywhere in the world.

Bitcoin is a form of digital money that has no middleman. Here's an example to explain how a simple bitcoin transaction works:

Jim and Jane using Bitcoin as digital money

Jane sells her car to Jim for £5,000 (1.18965 bitcoins at the time of writing) but wants Jim to pay her in bitcoin. To do this, Jim needs either:

1. Jane's **Bitcoin address.** This is a unique 26 to 35-character sequence made up of numbers and letters. It starts with the number 1 or 3. Or;

2. Jane's **QR code.** This is a unique bar code for Jane's Bitcoin address.

To save time, Jim goes with choice two.

Jane now opens a mobile **bitcoin wallet app** on her phone and gets to a screen that looks like this:

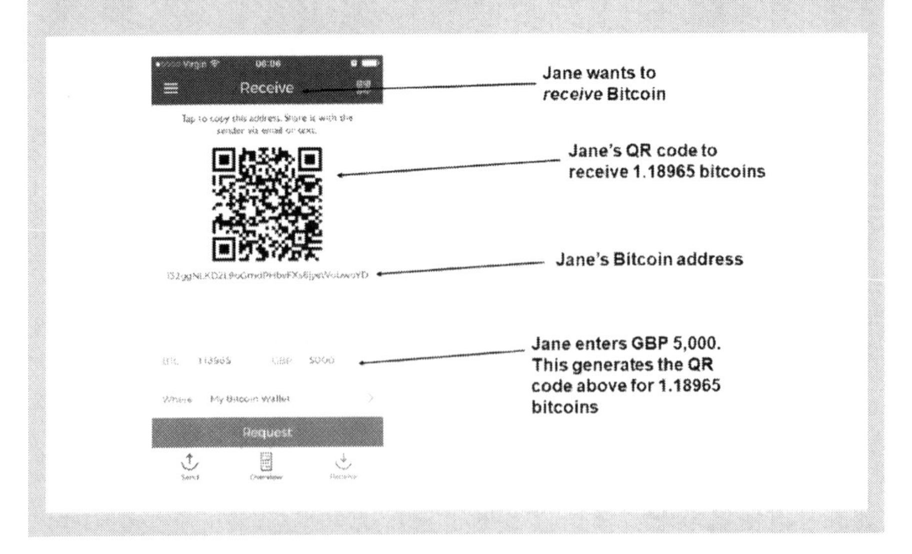

Jane wants to sell her car for GBP 5,000 worth of bitcoin. When she enters GBP 5,000, the app automatically generates a unique QR code for that amount in bitcoin - or BTC 1.18965.

Jane taps the **request button** at the bottom of her screen. Her phone now gives her the choice to send the BTC 1.18965 payment request (given by the unique QR code) to Jim by text message, email or WhatsApp.

Jim gets a text message from Jane with the payment request link. He clicks the link, which takes him to his own mobile bitcoin wallet app.

When Jim's app opens, he makes sure he's happy with the transaction before clicking **send**.

After about 10 minutes, Jane receives the BTC 1.18965 and hands Jim the car keys.

The point of the above example is just to explain the concept of a bitcoin transaction. We'll cover the different wallets and exchanges used for bitcoin and other cryptos in chapter fourteen.

The above example shows how simple it is to make a bitcoin transaction. Here are some bitcoin transaction news highlights from September 2017:

- **Texas real estate deal:** someone bought a property in Texas with bitcoin. The real estate broker, from Kuper Sotheby's International Realty, was surprised by how easy and fast it was[4].

- **South African supermarket:** South Africa's second largest supermarket, Pick n Pay, started accepting bitcoin at one of their stores in Cape Town[5].

- **London mansion sale:** a GBP 17 million mansion in Nottinghill went on sale for BTC 5,000[6]. Compare this to 2010, when Laszlo Hanyecz bought two pizzas for BTC 10,000!

The Bitcoin system

All bitcoin transactions are recorded and confirmed on the **Bitcoin blockchain.** This is a public online record (or ledger) of who bought what. Before transactions are confirmed on the blockchain, the global Bitcoin network, made up of computers from all over the world called **nodes**, records them in real time. Here's what the latest transactions look like on the blockchain:

Snapshot of the latest bitcoin transactions in real time (blockexplorer.com)

Latest Transactions

Hash	Value Out
caa9b63d3e18c93d703e8d79f0b9d3218cbc483b592...	0.12478484 BTC
30711efe1f8ce579c7612691f1f540d5f8f29816ee08...	0.01915604 BTC
e257be9d8b70178ed87151dd2c368362ac06565697...	10 BTC
2345f2da199b8eeb5b720938bc685a7065f233254f4...	0.01957954 BTC
11583593f47643aec404dde802e3d900bd0a7fa86ac...	1.6353946 BTC
dfe99a24e34dc0da3c33c43db9427ad93f3c711628bf...	0.12848752 BTC
7ed927eed3d7adf6337d9fcf72b3d6023d3bf942dc5...	0.94750961 BTC
32d9e59e3f354146bc4ea05af4fb6cddba3d1b4e6dc...	0.24304 BTC
79e11a895166b383302d0b118995737f2473fba0213...	86.4715503 BTC

If you go to ***www.blockexplorer.com*** *right now, you'll see new bitcoin transactions appearing and disappearing every second!*

The transactions form a **chain of ownership** (blockchain) on the bitcoin network. So, if Jane buys a motorbike from Tom with some of the bitcoins she got from Jim for the car, those bitcoin transactions are *chained together.*

Rather than record *who* was involved, the network produces a **hash** for each transaction. A hash is a unique encryption code used in cryptography - hence the word *crypto*currency.

Bitcoin **transaction hashing** is the process where data for each transaction is encrypted into a random string of letters and numbers (or a *hash*) as shown the screenshot on the last page.

More on hashing

Hashing is an encryption process which takes inputs and encrypts them (hashes them together) into a random string of outputs. For example, the word 'desk' (the input letters) could be hashed into the random output string 400s56xqlk.

The word desk is now encrypted into a hash (400s56xqlk). Anyone looking at the hash (400s56xqlk) would need a *specific key* to know the input (desk). Without that key, the hash is virtually impossible to decrypt, even with all the computing power in the world!

Four things about hashing make it good for cryptography:

1. It's easy to encrypt a message into a hash, but hard to do the reverse (hashes are 'one-way functions').

2. The same message (input) will always produce the same hash (output).

3. Small changes in the message cause big changes to the hash.

4. Two different messages can't have the same hash.

Bitcoin uses a hashing function called a **Secure Hashing Algorithm (SHA)**. SHA-01 was first developed by the US National Security Agency in 1995[7]. Bitcoin uses a much stronger version of SHA called **SHA-256**.

Bitcoin mining

The Bitcoin system groups recent bitcoin transactions together into **blocks.** Every ten minutes on average, a block is added the blockchain as part of the **bitcoin mining** process. This is how bitcoin transactions are confirmed without the need for a middleman such as a bank.

Bitcoin mining does two things:

1. It confirms blocks of transactions on the blockchain.

2. It creates new bitcoins for bitcoin miners.

To confirm each block of transactions on the blockchain, miners compete to solve a complex cryptographic puzzle. To do this, miners use Bitcoin mining software and vast computing power. Once a miner solves the next puzzle, other computers on the network (nodes) quickly verify the solution. A new block of transactions is then confirmed by the rest of the network and added to the blockchain. This process is called **Proof of Work (PoW).**

Solving the cryptographic puzzle is the hard part. Once a miner finds a solution, it's easy (and quick) for the rest of the Bitcoin network to verify it.

As a reward for finding the solution to the puzzle, which takes about ten minutes on average, the miner wins X number of bitcoins. At the time of writing, that miner wins 12.5 bitcoins after each block confirmation. This number halves every four years. With this maths[8], only 21 million bitcoins can ever be mined. This happens at a decreasing rate:

- Two-thirds of all bitcoins were already mined by 2015.

- 98% Of them will be mined by 2030.

- 99.8% Will be mined by 2040.

- The rest will be mined by 2140.

This finite supply makes bitcoin scarce, just like gold!

21 Million is not a large number when you consider how many trillions of dollars, pounds and euros are in circulation today. However, each bitcoin can be split into 100 million units to give 0.00000001 BTC or 1 **Satoshi**. Multiplying 21 million bitcoins by 100 million comes to 2.1 quadrillion Satoshis!

The **Bitcoin protocol** - the way the bitcoin system was designed to work - adjusts the difficulty of the puzzles over time so that it takes an average of ten minutes to confirm each block. Back in the day, the puzzles were easier, so they needed less computing power to do this. They're a lot harder now.

In 2009, you could mine 200 bitcoins with your home computer (CPU). But as the number of miners grew, so did mining competition. Miners soon needed stronger mining equipment to earn bitcoins, so they started using **General Processing Units (GPUs)** and then **ASIC Miners** ('Application-specific integrated circuit' mining equipment). It later became harder and less profitable for miners to mine on their own, so they teamed up to form **mining pools** that split the bitcoin profits.

Today *Bitmain* in China own two mining pools, Antpool and BTC.com, which together control over 30% of the entire Bitcoin network's processing power[9]. This is an issue with Bitcoin enthusiasts as it threatens decentralization of the blockchain. Decentralization is important for the future of Bitcoin as it helps ensure fair outcomes of **Bitcoin forks.** We will cover forks in detail in chapter five.

Bitcoin mining uses lots of electricity. In one of the most comprehensive studies of Bitcoin electricity consumption to date, Marc Bevand[10] asserts that Bitcoin mining consumes 8.27 terawatt-hours per year. This is more than Google, which uses 5.27 terawatt-hours[11], but less than the global production of cash and coins, at around 11 terawatt-hours[12]. Gold mining burns 132 terawatt-hours[13].

The Bitcoin Proof of Work (PoW) algorithm

Decrypting each transaction on its own is virtually impossible. But through the Bitcoin PoW, miners can unlock blocks of transactions every ten minutes on average. Let's now dive deeper into the technicalities behind this process.

To understand the Bitcoin PoW, you first need to understand what makes up a block on the blockchain. The diagram below shows conceptually what each block looks like:

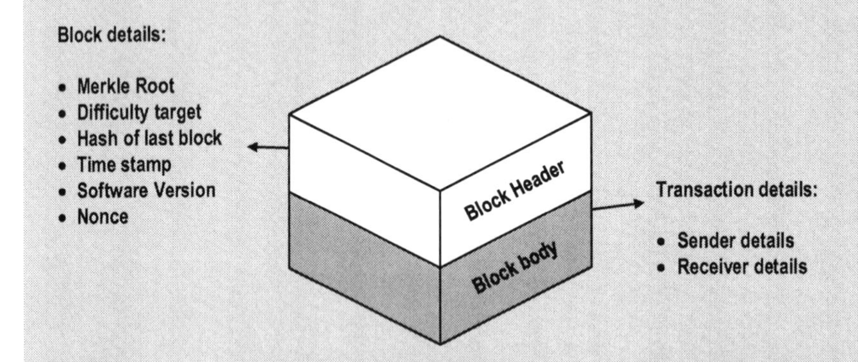

Each block has a **block header** and a **block body**. The block body stores the transaction details - you'll learn more about that in chapter five when we discuss **Bitcoin forks**.

For now, we focus on the block header. This has all the pieces miners need to solve the mining puzzle, so that they can add new blocks to the blockchain.

The first important thing in the block header is the **Merkle root**. Think of this as a digital signature for all the transactions within each block. Recall from earlier that each transaction has its own hash. As explained in the diagram opposite, each of these transaction hashes are then hashed together again and again to find the Merkle Root:

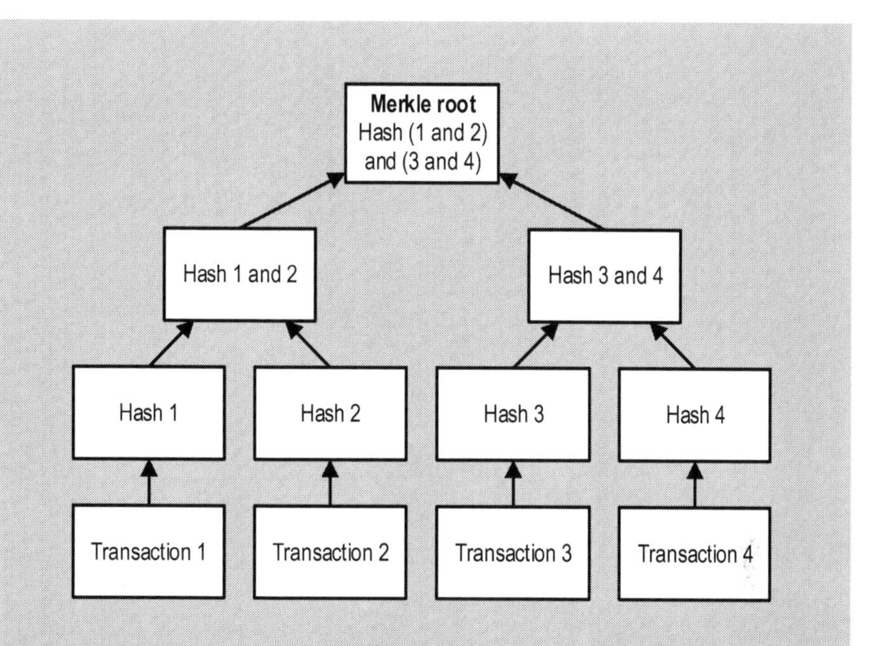

The next important thing in the block header is the **difficulty target**. This is a 64-character string of numbers and letters that starts with zeros. The difficulty target sets the difficulty of the mining puzzle.

Each block header also includes a **hash of the previous block before it** (hence the word blockchain). This is then hashed together with everything else in the block header to produce a second 64-character string of numbers.

As shown in the diagram over the page, if the value of that string of numbers is *less* than the value of the difficulty target, the block is unlocked and the mining puzzle is solved.

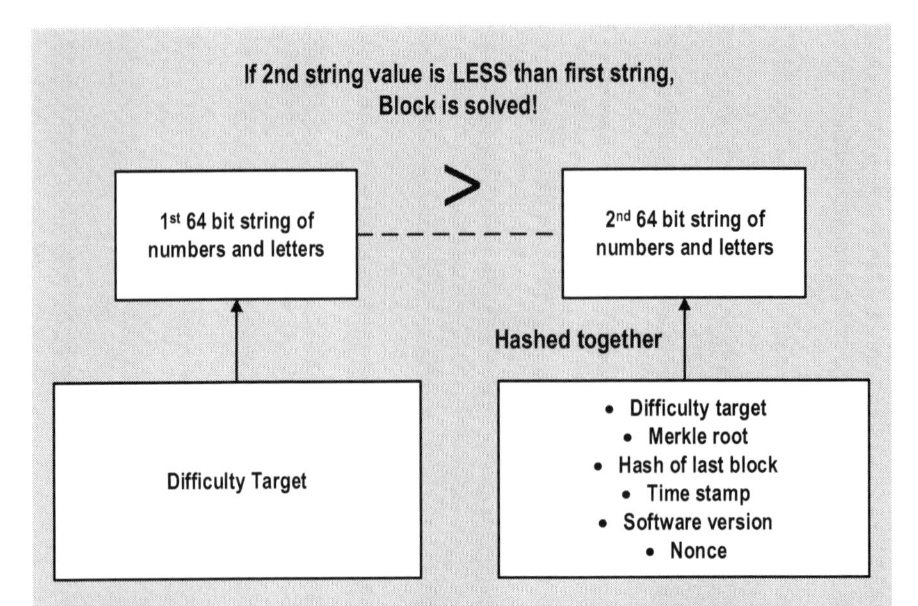

When miners first try solving the puzzle, the second-string value is higher than the value of the difficulty target. So, miners use something called a **nonce** to help them lower the value of the second string.

The mining software runs a hash on the block header billions of times, with the nonce adding a '1' to the input value of the hash each time. These tiny changes in inputs to the hashing algorithm cause large changes to the hash output value (up or down) of the second 64-character string.

After ten minutes (on average) of running the above process, a victorious miner finds a value for the second string that is less than the value of the difficulty target (first string). At this point, the puzzle is solved.

The solution to the puzzle is then quickly verified by the network, and the new block (along with all the block's transactions) are confirmed and added to the blockchain.

The next diagram shows how each block header links with the hash of the last block. This is how the blocks are chained together on the blockchain.

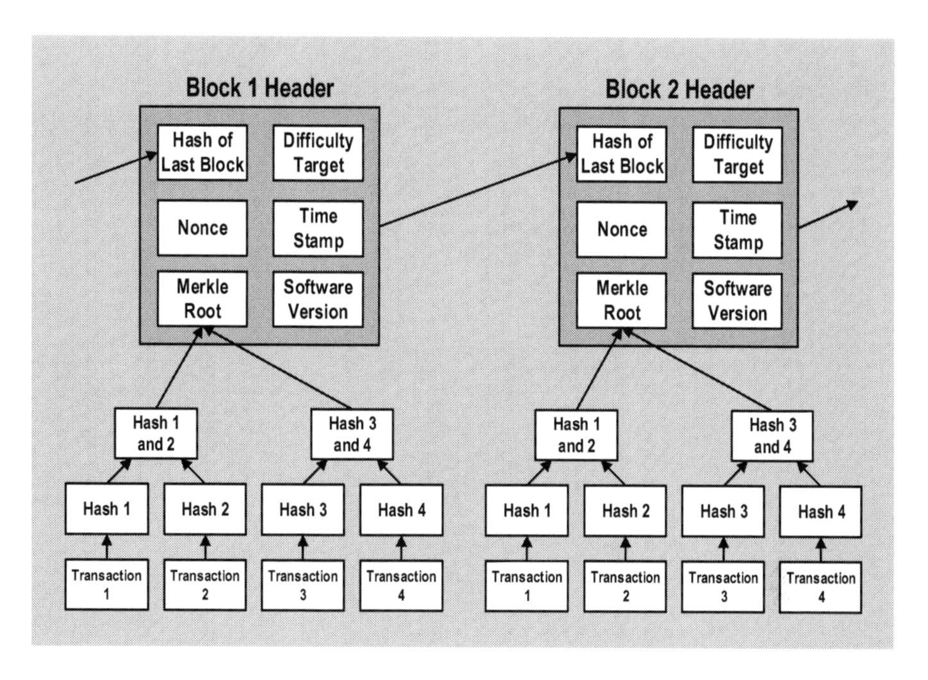

Once a block is mined through the process described above, it goes on the blockchain forever. The screen-print below shows what this looks like on blockchain.info, an online record of the Bitcoin blockchain:

<u>Bitcoin blocks mined in real time on blockchain.info</u>

Height	Time	Relayed By	Hash	Size (kB)
491855 (Main Chain)	2017-10-26 11:46:39	Unknown	[illegible]	238.01
491854 (Main Chain)	2017-10-26 11:44:33	Unknown	[illegible]	359.79
491853 (Main Chain)	2017-10-26 11:40:42	Unknown	[illegible]	1,006.12
491852 (Main Chain)	2017-10-26 11:36:23	Unknown	[illegible]	1,067.32
491851 (Main Chain)	2017-10-26 11:26:01	Unknown	[illegible]	1,044.39
491850 (Main Chain)	2017-10-26 11:23:26	Unknown	[illegible]	999.88
491849 (Main Chain)	2017-10-26 11:02:34	Unknown	[illegible]	1,072.51
491848 (Main Chain)	2017-10-26 10:50:10	Unknown	[illegible]	856.93
491847 (Main Chain)	2017-10-26 10:42:22	Unknown	[illegible]	116.18
491846 (Main Chain)	2017-10-26 10:40:14	Unknown	[illegible]	681.42

Notice above that the length of time taken to create each new block is shorter than or less than ten minutes. On average, each block takes ten minutes to mine, as the difficulty of solving each block adjusts.

Clicking on the top block - the 491,855th block in existence – displays the transactions in that block. It shows bitcoins being transferred between public Bitcoin addresses, but it doesn't show whom those addresses below to:

Bitcoin transactions inside block 491,855 on blockchain.info

Are Bitcoin transactions anonymous?

Bitcoin transactions are **pseudo-anonymous** (or disguised). I don't know who the addresses in the above screenshot belong to, and I'm not supposed to! Saying that, someone with a lot of time on their hands could try searching the blockchain for transaction patterns of a particular public Bitcoin address. If you know someone's address, you can see all the transactions they have ever made. This makes Bitcoin not as well suited to money laundering as many people believe!

Bitcoin transaction fees

One of the ideas behind blockchain was to lower transaction fees. This has been achieved with some of the cryptos you'll learn about in later chapters. But as I'll explain on the next page, Bitcoin fees are (currently) quite high.

Bitcoin developers are working hard to improve the Bitcoin system. Therefore, any current Bitcoin issues discussed in this book could be a thing of the past soon. As with any good cryptocurrency, Bitcoin is constantly evolving with time.

Bitcoin transaction fees are voluntarily paid by bitcoin transaction senders to miners as incentives for including transactions in a block. On top of receiving new bitcoins, the miner who solves the block is also rewarded all the transaction fees of that block. The problem here is that only a certain number of transactions can go in a single block. So, when lots of people are using Bitcoin, the forces of supply and demand for block space pushes up transaction fees.

The average transaction fee goes up with the value and demand for bitcoin and is now typically more than $5 per transaction, regardless of the transaction size[14]. This makes Bitcoin currently better suited for larger transactions than smaller ones.

Bitcoin transaction speed

The overcrowded blocks described above not only cause high fees for bitcoin transactions but also limit the number of transactions that Bitcoin can process at a time. This can often cause backlogs for bitcoin transactions, which makes Bitcoin slower than it should be.

At the time of writing, Bitcoin can only handle between three and four transactions per second[15]. This is a far cry from Visa, for example, which can process up to 24,000 transactions per second[16].

Bitcoin blocks have a capacity limit. Therefore, as more people use Bitcoin, the fees go up and the transaction speeds go down. At the same time, Bitcoin becomes more secure with each successive transaction. This tradeoff, as well as Bitcoin's limited supply, are why many people currently see bitcoin as a secure ***store of value*** *like gold, rather than a digital currency for small everyday transactions. We'll talk more about Bitcoin security on the next page.*

Is Bitcoin secure?

A common misconception is that Bitcoin is easy to hack, but the Bitcoin blockchain is safer than a Swiss bank account. There are two reasons for this:

1. Mining **secures** Bitcoin.

2. Game theory **enforces** Bitcoin.

Recall that Bitcoin **miners** try finding a hash of the block header that is smaller than the value of the difficulty target. Once the Bitcoin network confirms a block after this process is successful, the transactions in that block go on the Bitcoin blockchain. This is the *first* confirmation of those transactions.

The blocks are then layered on top of each other over and over in a **chain of blocks** (blockchain). As time goes on, each new block adds extra confirmations to *all* the previous blocks before it. In other words, as time goes on, transactions become exponentially harder to reverse. This is why it's so hard to spend the same bitcoin twice.

After the first block is confirmed on the blockchain, a network attacker would need more than half the computing power of the entire Bitcoin network to reverse the block and any transactions within it. This is known as a **51% attack**. While these are theoretically possible, they are highly unlikely to happen.

After six consecutive block confirmations - which takes about an hour at an average of ten minutes per block - it is mathematically impossible for a 51% attacker to reverse any of the transactions in a block.

Nick Szabo, who developed the concept of ***smart contracts*** *(covered in chapter four), described blockchain as "a fly trapped in amber" in one of Tim Ferris's most listened to podcasts[17]. Each time a block is confirmed, another layer of amber is added on top of the fly. In this scenario, the fly is a transaction. The more amber is added on top of it, the harder it is for the fly to get out.*

51% Attacks can only occur - if at all - after a block has been mined. But what about the potential for a network attack *before* a block has been mined?

A **Finney attack** is when a miner tries to spend the same bitcoins twice before mining a block.

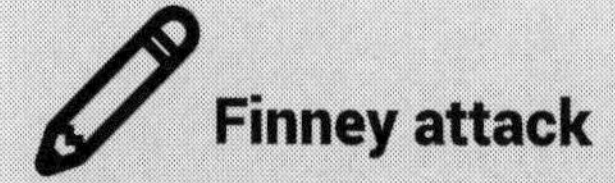

Finney attack

Fred uses a Finney attack to download the latest crypto day trading course from *gauranteedcryptoreturns.com* without paying for it. The course costs 2 BTC because it 'guarantees' a 700% yearly investment return!

While mining *block X*, Fred sends 2 BTC to one of his own Bitcoin addresses. Fred does *not* broadcast this transaction to the Bitcoin network.

Fortunately for Fred, his mining software solves the cryptographic puzzle of block X before any other miner. Once the network has confirmed Fred's solution, he will win block X and the bitcoin rewards that go with it.

Normally, Fred's mining rig would broadcast his victory out to the network straight away. But because Fred is a **Finney attacker**, he quickly buys the course from gauranteedcryptoreturns.com and instantly downloads it.

Fred now broadcasts to the Bitcoin network that he has mined block X. Instead of broadcasting the 2 BTC crypto course transaction, he broadcasts the 2 BTC he sent to himself.

Therefore, the 2 BTC that Fred was supposed to pay the company is not confirmed on the blockchain, so the payment never went through. He has **spent the same bitcoins twice.**

Fred downloaded the trading course without paying the 2 BTC to the merchant, Gauranteedcryptoreturns, who is the Finney attack victim. But with a name like that, they probably deserved it anyway!

Finney attacks like the one described above are highly unlikely to happen. For a Finney attack to be successful:

1. **The seller must process the sale before it is confirmed on the blockchain for the first time.** After one block confirmation, a Finney attack is impossible. Sellers can easily protect themselves from Finney attacks by waiting for one block confirmation before releasing a sale.

2. **The product must be instantly downloadable.** If the crypto course was posted by mail, the company would have no reason to deliver it after not receiving payment confirmation on the blockchain.

3. **The timing must be perfect for the Finney attacker.** First, Fred had to mine the block. Second, he had 'buy' and instantly download the course before the network found out. He would only have seconds to do this.

4. **The juice must be worth the squeeze.** Finney attacks are a lot of work for the miner. The crypto course would need to deliver on its promise of a 700% return each year for the attack to be worth the effort!

Other Bitcoin attacks are Race attacks, Vector 76 attacks and Alternative History attacks. These all try to spend the same Bitcoin twice at the expense of the merchant. Merchants can take precautions to significantly reduce the risks of each type of attack happening to them. Like Finney and 51% attacks, they're also a complete waste of time and resources for the attacker.

Bitcoin and Game Theory

In the movie *A Beautiful Mind*, Russell Crowe plays John Nash, the man who invented **game theory**. In one scene, Nash is sitting at a table in a bar drinking beer with four of his classmates.

A beautiful woman walks into the bar. Nash has an epiphany: if they all compete for her, they will all get shut down. But if they all ignore her and approach the other women standing next to her, then none of them will leave the bar alone.

Nash was referring to a type of game theory where individuals achieve the best outcome for themselves by doing what's best for the group.

This applies to Bitcoin.

Miners get the best result (bitcoin profits) when they do what's right for the Bitcoin network. A 51% attack, for example, would cost the attacker billions of dollars in computing power. All the attacker would get for this is being able to double spend *one* transaction. This is hardly the best result.

Even if the attacker was successful – which is highly unlikely - the Bitcoin network would pick up the crime and at once remove the attacker from the network. So, the attacker would be short billions of dollars for zero results.

The attacker is therefore much better off mining bitcoins the way the network intended. The potential reward of bitcoins and transaction fees incentivizes the miner to play by the rules!

Final words on Bitcoin

Before I took the time to learn about cryptos, I believed in some of the FUD. In crypto slang, FUD means having "fear, uncertainty and doubt" about the future of cryptos.

I was not alone.

When most people first heard about Bitcoin they were equally sceptical, and thought it a fad for hipsters, a Ponzi scheme for charlatans, or a money laundering machine for drug dealers and terrorists.

Bitcoin may still be some of those things, but it's going mainstream fast. Once people understand how it works, they usually become positive about it's potential (and that of other cryptos) to change the financial system for the *better* - not the worse.

Bitcoin was the first use of blockchain. It may not be perfect right now, but it's a pretty good start!

Chapter Summary

1. *Bitcoin is both a decentralized blockchain system (Bitcoin with a large "B") and a digital form of money (bitcoin with a small "b"). It was the first blockchain and the first cryptocurrency.*

2. *SHA-256 cryptography secures bitcoin transactions. Transactions are grouped together into blocks.*

3. *Every ten minutes on average, transaction blocks are added to the blockchain through the Proof of Work (PoW) mining process, where miners compete to solve cryptographic puzzles. If they win, miners are rewarded new bitcoins and all the transaction fees for the block.*

4. *Transaction fees are voluntary but are driven by the supply and demand for block space. If Bitcoin blocks get overcrowded, and you want a bitcoin transaction to go through on time, you may need to pay up!*

5. *Mining creates new bitcoins. The number of bitcoins in the world increases at a decreasing rate. 21 Million bitcoins can only ever be mined. This will happen in the year 2140. This gives Bitcoin scarcity, like gold.*

6. *Bitcoin is extremely secure. The longer a transaction stays on the blockchain, the harder it is to reverse.*

7. *Bitcoin's high transaction fees, slow transaction time, extreme security and finite supply make it currently better suited as a store of value, like gold, rather than as a currency for smaller transactions. However, this could change with ongoing work by developers.*

CHAPTER 3

BITCOIN ALTERNATIVES: OTHER TYPES OF CRYPTO MONEY

"So the reason why people use Litecoin over Bitcoin for everyday purchases is because the transactions fees are lower and it's also a faster payment turnover"

Charlie Lee

Before 2011, Bitcoin was the only blockchain based cryptocurrency. Then new coins started popping up all over the place. Soon there was Namecoin, IOcoin, Ixcoin, Solidcoin, Solidcoin2 and Geistheld - all bad spinoffs of Satoshi's original work. Then came Litecoin, Dash, Monero and Ripple, each stamping their mark in the crypto community as digital forms of money.

Litecoin (LTC)

Charlie Lee launched **Litecoin** in October 2011[18]. He cleverly marketed it as the "silver to bitcoin's gold". As the name suggests, Litecoin is a 'lighter' version of Bitcoin. Litecoin is like Bitcoin in many ways but could work better for everyday transactions, like buying a cup of coffee. This is because it is currently faster and has lower transaction fees than Bitcoin.

Here are two key differences between Litecoin and Bitcoin:

1. Litecoin uses a different Proof of Work (PoW) algorithm to Bitcoin, called **scrypt.**

   Recall from the last chapter that competition amongst Bitcoin miners caused them to use more powerful and expensive mining equipment as time went on. Initially, Bitcoin miners used ordinary computers (CPUs) to mine bitcoins. They then upgraded to General Processing Units (GPUs) before later using ASIC Miners.

   Lee wanted to lower the barriers to entry for Litecoin miners, so he chose to use a scrypt PoW algorithm. Scrypt works in a similar way to Bitcoin's SHA-256 PoW algorithm covered in the last chapter, except it relies more on computer memory to solve, and less on computer processing power. At the time, this made Litecoin mining more accessible for ordinary miners, as they could mine Litecoins with their home computers.

   As with Bitcoin, competition amongst Litecoin miners has increased with time. Today there are AISCs for Litecoin.

2. **It takes an average of 2.5 minutes to mine a Litecoin block** instead of 10 minutes like it does for Bitcoin. In light of this, Litecoin also has four times the maximum supply of Bitcoin - or 84 million litecoins.

Dash (DASH)

Evan Duffield started Dash in January 2014. Duffield first named it XCoin, then Darkcoin, before he changed it to Dash in March 2014[19]. Unlike Litecoin, Dash is very different to Bitcoin for three reasons:

1. Transactions can be instantly confirmed (in 1.3 seconds)[20] with the Dash **instant send** option.

2. Transactions can be made private with the Dash **private send** option.

3. Dash runs itself like a business; it was the first **Decentralized Autonomous Organization (DAO).**

1. Dash instant transaction confirmations

With Bitcoin and most other cryptocurrencies, transactions are confirmed on the blockchain once a new block has been mined. Since this takes 2.5 minutes on average for Litecoin and 10 minutes on average for Bitcoin, transactions are not instantly confirmed.

Dash gets around this with its **instant send** option, which uses **masternodes** to instantly confirm transactions. Dash users can choose if they want to use instant send. If they choose not to use it, Dash transactions take about 2.5 minutes on average to confirm.

Recall from chapter two that a node is any computer used on the blockchain network. Masternodes are nodes with more responsibilities than regular nodes - they oversee the entire Dash network.

Unlike Bitcoin or Litecoin, Dash is a two-tier network. The first tier is made up of miners, who mine transactions with Dash mining software through Proof of Work (PoW). The second tier consists of *super users*, who oversee the Dash network with their masternodes by:

- Instantly confirming Dash transactions (1.3 seconds).

- Shuffling Dash transactions to make them more private - something we'll go on the next page.

Anyone can become a masternode if they own 1,000 Dash. At the time of writing, that's worth over $500,000! In return, masternode users receive commissions paid in Dash for overseeing the Dash network. Per the Dash website, these commissions are estimated to be around 10% per year[21].

Since masternodes have a lot to lose if things go wrong, they are incentivized to act in the best interests of the Dash network. If they don't, they compromise the Dash network. This would lower the price of all the Dash they own, as well as the value of their Dash commissions. This is another example of crypto game theory at play!

The masternode system is known as **Proof of Service (PoSe)**. Dash uses PoW for the first tier of its network (miners) and PoSe for the second tier (masternodes).

Dash instant send

As with Litecoin, each Dash block takes 2.5 minutes on average to mine. But even though the Dash average block time is the same speed as Litecoin's, Dash transactions can be instantly confirmed. Dash achieves this through its instant send process.

Each new Dash block randomly chooses 10 masternodes to make instant confirmations. If Jean spends some Dash, her transaction is at once confirmed and **locked** by those 10 masternodes.

At the same time, the other Dash nodes keep mining the Dash blocks. About an hour later, the masternodes unlock Jean's transaction. By that time, around forty block confirmations have already happened – and Jean's transaction is confirmed forever on the Dash blockchain.

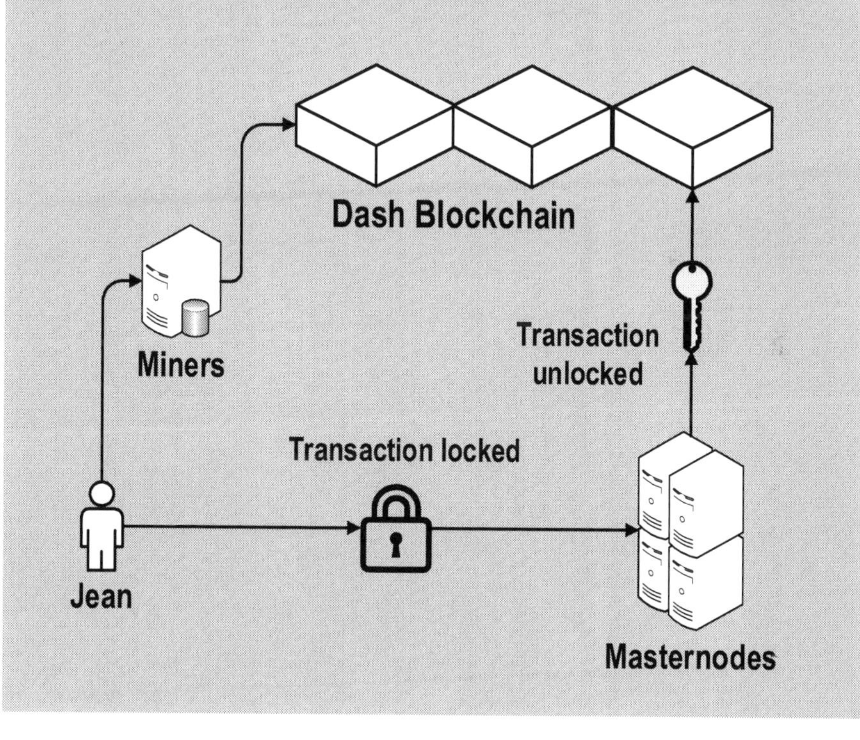

2. Dash and Privacy

As mentioned in the last chapter, bitcoin transactions are not completely private – they are **pseudo-anonymous**. If I send you bitcoins, our personal details can't be seen on the Bitcoin blockchain. But if money keeps going from my address to your address, people could notice a pattern.

And if someone knows your public Bitcoin address, they could (if they really wanted to) inspect the blockchain to see every Bitcoin address you have ever transacted with. They can also look up your bitcoin balance!

Pseudo-anonymity is good for making sure money doesn't get used for the wrong reasons. But it won't protect people in oppressed countries from governments who steel citizen's hard-earned money to fill their own pockets. Nor would it protect companies from having confidential revenue information fall into the wrong hands. As explained in the box below, pseudo-anonymity is also bad for the **fungibility** of a currency.

What is fungibility?

A currency is fungible if each of its units have the same value. For example, if a money launderer makes bitcoin transactions through a crypto exchange and the exchange finds out, they might freeze his account. Therefore, the money launderer wouldn't be able to sell his bitcoins.

Because he can't sell them, the money launder's bitcoins are worth less than all the other bitcoins. The currency is not **fungible** because some coins are worth different amounts to others. If this happens often enough, the overall value of bitcoin goes down.

Paper money is fungible because there is no record of where that money came from.

A 10-pound note is the same as any other 10-pound note.

Dash users have the **private send** option in their Dash wallets to send transactions privately. This could make Dash more fungible than bitcoin. In other words, when transactions are private, it's harder for Dash to be tainted on the blockchain by whomever last owned them.

As long as transactions remain private, every Dash coin is worth the same.

Dash private send

With *private send,* masternodes shuffle transactions together before they hit the blockchain. If Jean sends Dash to someone and chooses the private send option, her transaction is grouped with the transactions of other people, as shown in the below diagram...

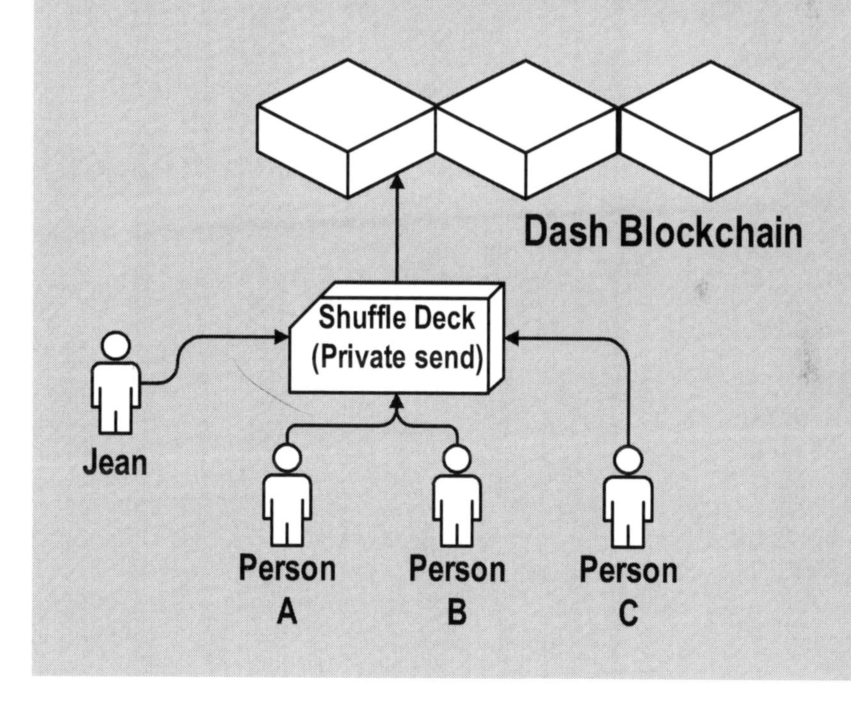

3. Decentralized Autonomous Organization (DAO)

Dash runs like a business. Normally with cryptocurrencies, miners get all the rewards for securing and supporting the network by mining the blocks. With Dash, the rewards are split three ways[22]:

- Miners get 45%.
- Masternodes get 45%.
- The **treasury** gets 10%.

The treasury is made up of people who want Dash to do well. This includes developers, marketers and **Dash contractors**. If someone wants to improve Dash, they can send a proposal to the Dash network at www.dash.org/governance. The masternodes then vote on the proposal. If it gets approved, that person is paid in Dash for their contribution to the Dash network.

The treasury and masternode system is what makes Dash run like a business - or a **Decentralized Autonomous Organization (DAO)**. This has caused division amongst the crypto community:

- Some like the DAO because it gives Dash more funding to improve.

- Others don't like it because it goes against the core foundations of pure peer-to-peer decentralization.

Monero (XMR)

As is the case with Bitcoin, it's a mystery as to who created Monero. We do however know that the creator went by the username thankful_for_today on bitcointalk.org[23]. Monero was created in April 2014 (originally named Bitmonero) and is now one of the world's most private cryptocurrencies[2]. Unlike Dash:

- Monero doesn't have masternodes that might 'see' transactions.
- Monero is private by default, while Dash users have the option to use Dash private send.

Monero has four things that give it great privacy:

1. **Stealth addresses** to hide the Monero receiver.
2. **Ring signatures** to hide the Monero spender.
3. **Ring confidential transactions** to hide the transaction amount.
4. **I2P addresses** to mask the internet address of the Monero user.

1. Monero Stealth Addresses

Each Monero transaction has a unique **stealth address**, which hides the true wallet address of the person receiving a Monero payment. Anyone can see the stealth address on the Monero blockchain, but only the sender and receiver know about the transaction.

If James sends Amy Monero, an observer of the Monero blockchain would see money going to an unknown Monero address. Since that address is a stealth address, the observer cannot link it to Amy nor James.

---

[2] Cryptocurrencies like ZCash and Verge also offer high privacy levels. To keep this book from being too long, I don't cover them all, but please see the back of this book for recommendations to resources where you can learn more.

Amy has a special **private view key**, which scans the blockchain for the transaction. Once her private view key finds the stealth address associated with the transaction, it unlocks it, and Amy gets the monero that James sent to her.

As you'll learn in this chapter, Monero transactions are completely private. This would of course be a problem for governments, auditors and regulators. To get around this, the Monero team developed a ***public view key****, which Monero users can give to whomever they choose. A view key lets other people see that user's Monero transactions.*

2. Monero Ring Signatures

Ring signatures mask the true Monero sender by grouping each sender with other past senders from the Monero blockchain.

Monero Ring Signatures explained

When James sends Monero to Amy, his address is grouped with other senders to generate a single signature called a **ring signature**. On the Monero Blockchain, it will look like Amy's address received Monero from lots of different senders even though she only received the Monero from James.

Remember, Monero generates a new stealth address for each transaction on top of this, which makes it even harder for an outside observer to know where the transaction came from. The next picture shows what this would look like on the Monero blockchain:

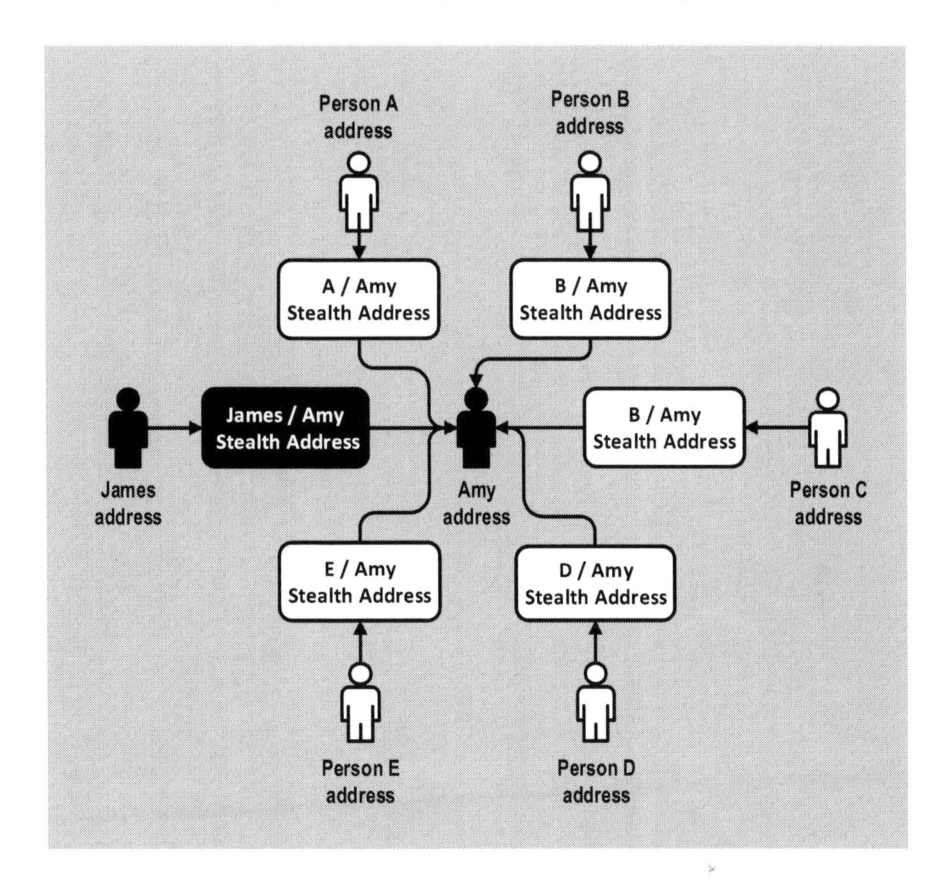

3. Ring Confidential Transactions (Ring CT)

Monero also hides transaction amounts through a similar process to ring signatures described above. If James sends Amy 10 XMR, the blockchain would just show random amounts.

4. I2P Addresses

The Monero team are developing project **Kovri**. This will prevent anyone from knowing the internet IP address of the Monero user in the first place.

Ripple (XRP)

Brad Garlinghouse, the CEO of Ripple, often jokes how flying money across the globe on an aeroplane is faster than using the international banking system[24]. Ripple solves this problem.

Ripple is two things:

1. A payment system.
2. A cryptocurrency.

1. Ripple as a payment system

The Ripple system works for *fiat currencies* (government-backed money like dollars, pounds and euros) as well as other cryptocurrencies besides ripple (XRP). Let's first go over what happens with currencies other than XRP.

The Ripple system is based on IOU's (I owe you). In other words, within the Ripple system, money isn't actually transferred from one place to another - only the promise of payment is transferred. As with any IOU, you need to trust the person who sends you the IOU. So, if you send me an IOU for $20, I need to trust you enough to know that you will eventually pay me that $20.

To solve the trust issue, Ripple works like the **Hawala system[25].** This is a non-digital trust-based system for transferring money based on IOU's. The Hawala system first started in ancient South-East Asia but is still used today, often by immigrants living in developed countries, to send money home to their families without paying huge transaction costs.

The example on the next page shows how the Hawala system works...

Dave pays Kate through the Hawala system

Dave, who lives in town A, wants to send $100 to Kate, who lives in town B. To do this, Dave gives $100 to his Hawala dealer (Dealer A), along with a password that Kate knows.

Next, Dave's Hawala dealer calls Kate's Hawala dealer (Dealer B) to say that Dave wants to send Kate $100. Dealer B calls Kate and asks for the password. Since Kate knows the password, Dealer B gives Kate the $100.

Dealer A and Dealer B *trust* each other. Dealer B, now short $100, records that Dave's Hawala dealer, Dealer A, owes him $100.

Finally, dealer B calls dealer A to confirm the transaction. Dealer A now updates his own records to say he owes $100 to Dealer B. The below diagram sums up this process:

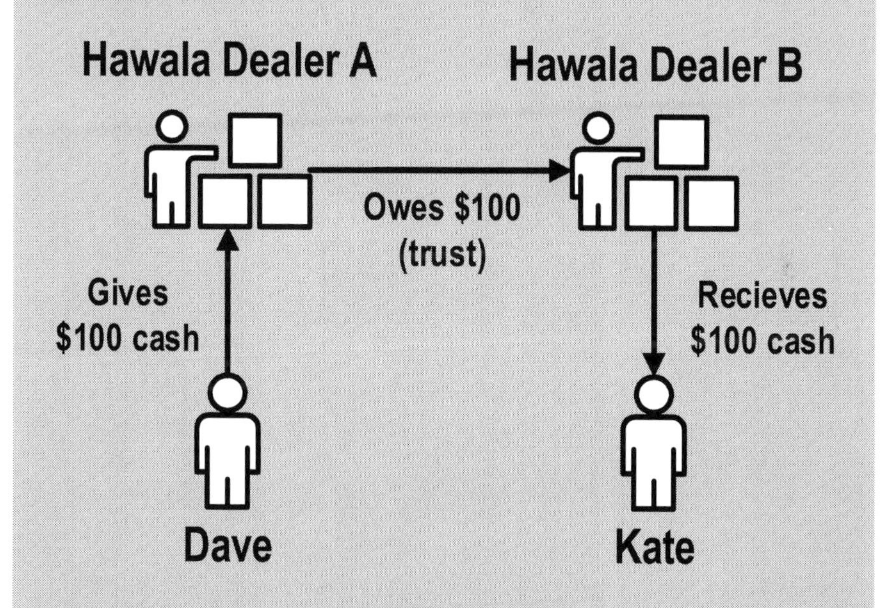

The key point here is that the Hawala system only works if the Hawala dealers trust each other!

Ripple runs much like the Hawala system except instead of Hawala dealers, there are **Ripple gateways**. These are usually banks or financial companies. It's good for them to be part of the Ripple network because it's good for their customers, who gain access to Ripple's faster and cheaper international payment services.

But Ripple is a huge network, so not everyone using Ripple knows and trusts one another. To fix this, Ripple uses **chains of trusts** to interconnect Ripple gateways. As shown in the next diagram, there can be indirect links of trust between the gateways:

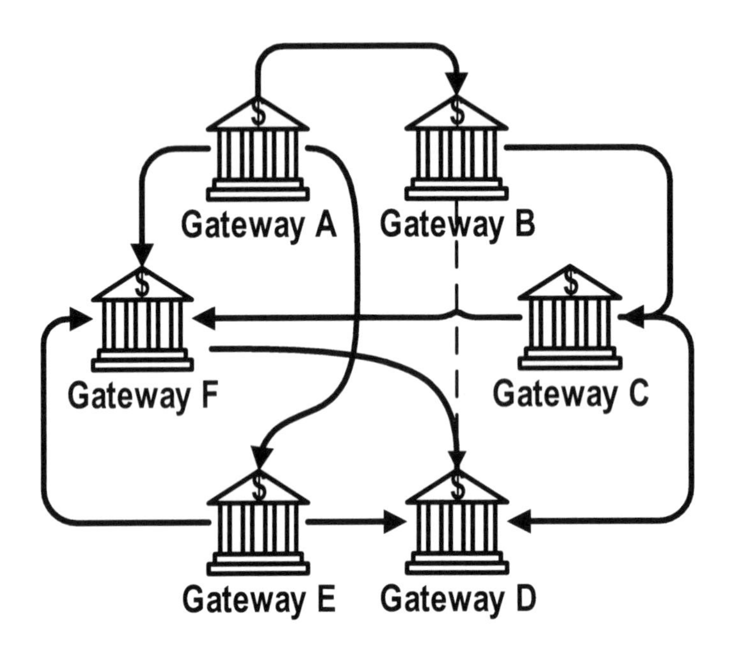

Since gateway B doesn't directly trust gateway D, there is no solid line directly connecting them to each other. However, gateway B trusts gateway C, which trusts gateway D, so there is an indirect link (dotted line) of trust from B to D.

The trust is *rippled* across the network.

Ripple gateways transport payment IOU information to each other using **https:** the same protocol that banks already use for secure online credit card payments. Five to ten seconds after a payment is made, the Ripple network triggers the gateways involved in the transaction to update their ledgers.

Just before that, Ripple updates the state of its own **decentralized Ripple blockchain** to reflect who owns what. But instead of miners confirming transactions, the state of the blockchain is very quickly agreed by a **consensus process** amongst the computers in the Ripple network.

2. Ripple as a cryptocurrency (XRP)

The Ripple network can be used for any type of currency or asset that Ripple gateways are willing to accept. Ripple the cryptocurrency (XRP) is *one* of the currencies used for the Ripple system. If the network can't find a chain of trust between two Ripple gateways (if there were no dotted or solid line connecting them in the diagram on the last page), then the two gateways can transact with XRP. While other currencies used by the Ripple system are based on the IOU Hawala system, the gateways actually send and receive XRP.

So, if Dave sends Kate XRP through the network, he is actually sending XRP to Kate, rather than an IOU through one of the Ripple gateways. Because everyone using Ripple agrees to use XRP, the gateways involved in the transaction don't need to trust each other.

More on Ripple

Ripple has come under fire from the crypto community because it is not decentralized in the same way as other cryptocurrencies like Bitcoin, Litecoin and Monero (and to a lesser extent Dash) - it relies on big banks and financial institutions working together to exchange value.

Added to this, it is estimated that around 60% of the XRP supply is owned by Ripple the company[26]. Therefore, Ripple has the power to control the supply of XRP in the market, giving it a degree of control over its price[3].

---

[3] Because the Ripple company own so much XRP, they could in theory crash the price if they sold all of it. This would not be in the interests of Ripple, however.

Across the world, banks like UBS, MUFG, Santander and Credit Agricole (to name a few) already use the Ripple System (rather than XRP the cryptocurrency) to transfer payments[27]. Before Ripple, most banks used the SWIFT payment system. SWIFT is an old technology which takes much longer for international payments.

Like SWIFT, Ripple follows banking regulations. Ripple is also a better technology than SWIFT, so there is no reason for SWIFT to stay ahead of Ripple as the core system for international banking payments. That said, the extent to which XRP the cryptocurrency becomes widely used by banks in the future remains to be seen.

Like Litecoin, Ripple sees itself as a complement to Bitcoin. The Ripple payments system works for bitcoin and other cryptocurrencies.

On that note, we'll look at smart contracts in the next chapter. This should give you a glimpse into the true potential of blockchain technology...

Chapter Summary

1. *Bitcoin was the first blockchain based cryptocurrency. It proved that blockchain is a good idea.*
2. *Since Bitcoin, many other blockchain based payment systems have been created. Some good, some not so good.*
3. *Litecoin is a lot like Bitcoin but is currently faster and has lower fees. This makes it currently better suited to smaller transactions than Bitcoin.*
4. *Privacy is important for fungibility. Dash is more private than Bitcoin because of its private send option. Dash runs like a business and has masternodes to speed things up.*
5. *Monero is more private than Dash because it hides transaction senders and receivers, transaction amounts and user IP addresses.*
6. *The Ripple network works like the Hawala payment system and is used by banks to send money to each other faster and more cheaply than they can with SWIFT. Ripple the cryptocurrency (XRP) is used in the Ripple system when there are no direct or indirect links of trust between two Ripple gateways.*

CHAPTER 4

ETHEREUM, SMART CONTRACTS AND DAPPS

"When I came up with Ethereum, my first thought was, 'Okay, this thing is too good to be true.'"

Vitalik Buterin

Bitcoin and other cryptocurrencies cut the middleman out of simple financial transactions. They are digital money without banks, financial institutions or governments behind them. Instead, all transactions are processed and confirmed with decentralized blockchains.

Ethereum takes things up a notch.

Vitalik Buterin first came up with Ethereum[28] in 2013. Vitalik was born in Russia in 1994 before moving to Canada. As the legend goes, his distrust of centralization started from an early age, when Blizzard Entertainment lowered the damage per second of one of his World of Warcraft character's spells without his permission[29].

Ethereum is two things:

1. A world computer that no one controls.

2. A one size fits all blockchain that different decentralized applications can be built on top of.

If Bitcoin was a telephone, Ethereum would be a smartphone with all the apps. With a telephone, you can send information (your voice) to the person on the other line. You can do this with your smartphone too, but you can also use lots of different mobile apps. These apps let you do all kinds of things, like go on Facebook, listen to music on Spotify, trade the stock market, send and receive crypto payments and even play Angry Birds.

Sticking with the above analogy, Bitcoin uses blockchain for simple financial transactions. Ethereum does this too, but programmers can also build **dApps** (decentralized apps) on the Ethereum blockchain. We'll explore dApps later in this chapter, but first, let's learn more about Ethereum transactions.

Ethereum transactions

With Bitcoin and many other cryptocurrencies, there are two types of user accounts in a transaction: senders and receivers. With Ethereum, there is also a third user account: **smart contracts.**

Like senders and receivers, smart contracts have their own unique Ethereum addresses. This means that they can transact on the Ethereum blockchain, just like you and me.

Smart contracts are lines of code that developers can upload to the Ethereum blockchain. They give a set of rules to decide the outcome of a transaction. Once those rules are programmed to the blockchain, they are agreed by the Ethereum network and can't be changed.

The Ethereum token is known as **ether (ETH)**. Smart contracts aren't needed for simple ether transactions. I could send ether from my Ethereum address to yours without one, just like I could send you bitcoin. But if I wanted *conditions* attached to the payment, I could send ether to a smart contract first. The smart contract would then pay you the ether *if* those conditions are met.

The picture over the page can help you visualize this. Here, smart contracts go in the middle of the sender and the receiver. The receiver only gets paid *if* the conditions programmed into the smart contract are met. If the conditions are not met, the ETH could stay at the smart contract address or go back to the sender. This all depends on the how the smart contract was originally programmed.

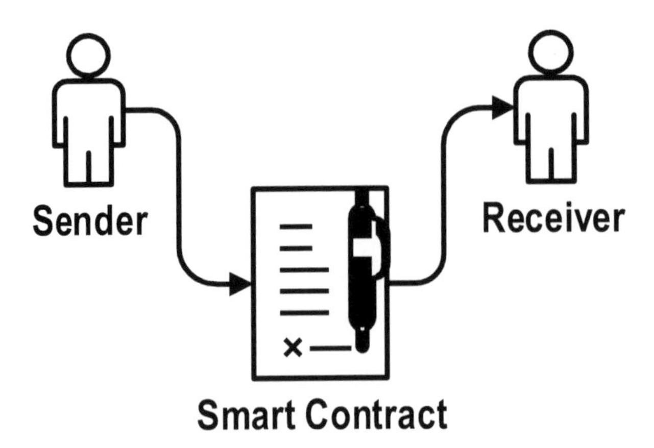

There are endless ways that smart contracts can be programmed to interact with senders and receivers on the Ethereum blockchain. Not only that, but smart contracts can also be programmed to interact with each other. This means they could become the norm for insurance payouts, legal contracts, financial derivatives, share certificates, election voting, crowdfunding, automated investing and much more.

Ethereum, therefore, is an outstanding technological breakthrough. It is an automated, decentralized and global database of programmable rules and outcomes that no single person, government or company controls.

Ethereum smart contracts

Nick and Mike are developers who know how to program smart contracts to the Ethereum blockchain. They are also rugby fans. Every Saturday, they watch a rugby game together at their local pub and bet on the result.

But there's a problem. When Nick's team loses, he often makes an excuse not to pay Mike. When Mike's team loses, he has excuses of his own. Their rugby bets are a bit of a joke, as neither Nick nor Mike trust each other to pay up if the other one loses.

One Saturday afternoon, they decide to put an end to their useless bets once and for all. They build a smart contract with three conditions:

1. If Nick's team wins, Mike pays Nick 1 ETH.
2. If Mike's team wins, Nick pays Mike 1 ETH.
3. If the game is a draw, Nick and Mike both get their money back.

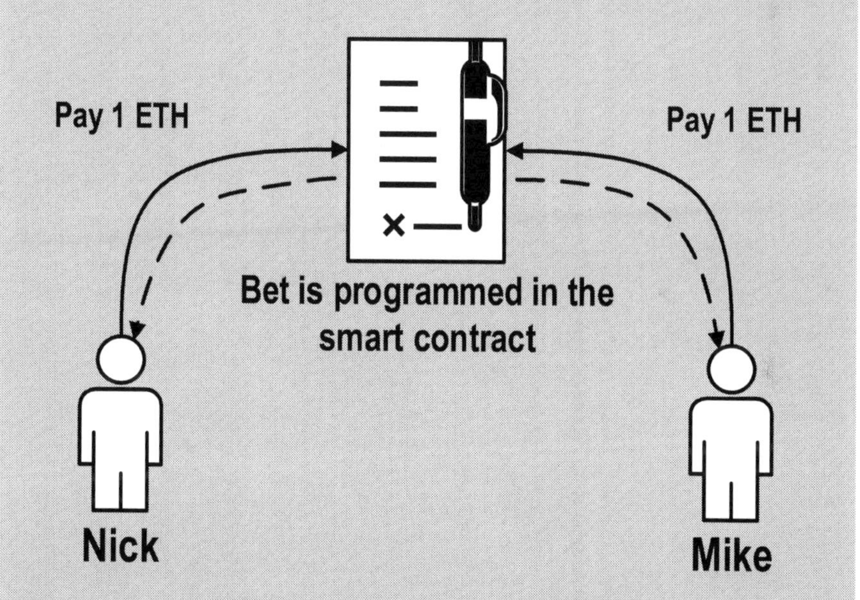

They upload the smart contract to the Ethereum blockchain and each send 1 ETH to the smart contract address. Now, the conditions of the bet cannot be altered!

You may be wondering how the smart contract could know the result of the match. One way to do this would be to have a neutral party (for example Nick and Mike's bartender) act as an **Oracle**.

An Oracle is needed where information can't be found on the blockchain itself. In this case, the Oracle would need to send another 'transaction' to the smart contract with the match result. Of course, Nick and Mike would need to trust their bartender to report the result correctly.

To solve this potential trust issue, the Oracle could be a sports related website or even a decentralized network of mediators that vote on the real result. An example of this is the **Augur** dApp, which we will go over shortly.

Ethereum mining

Like Bitcoin, Ethereum uses a Proof of Work (PoW) mining algorithm. Miners are rewarded 5 ethers if they win the block and new blocks are mined every 15 seconds on average[30]. Overall, somewhere between 10 and 15 million ethers are mined each year[31].

Ethereum mining confirms transactions to the Ethereum blockchain. It also confirms the **state** of smart contracts. For example, one state could be 'Nick's rugby team won, so Mike owes Nick 1 ETH'. The next state of the smart contract could be 'Mike has paid Nick 1 ETH; the bet is settled'.

Ethereum PoW and smart contract states

Recall from chapter two that the Bitcoin Proof of Work (PoW) uses a **Merkle tree** to hash transaction data together to find a **Merkle root.** For the PoW puzzle, the block header is hashed billions of times using a nonce until the hash of the block header is less than the value of the difficulty target. Ethereum uses a similar process to confirm simple ETH transactions to its blockchain.

However, Ethereum's blockchain also needs a way to store **smart contract states**. To do this, it needs another Merkle tree called a **Merkle Patricia Tree.** Unlike 'simple' Merkle trees, Merkle Patricia Trees can handle changing states.

The technical explanation of how Merkle Patricia Trees work is far beyond the scope of this book (and most books for that matter!). But if you like, you can read it in the words of Vitalik Buterin himself at the link below:

https://blog.ethereum.org/2015/11/15/merkling-in-ethereum.

Ethereum transaction fees

As mentioned earlier, miners win 5 ethers if they solve the Ethereum PoW puzzle. They also charge small fees for each transaction (or step) in each smart contract. A complicated smart contract with many steps would have higher fees than a simple smart contract with fewer steps.

Whatever the fees, miners charge them in **gas** rather than ether. You can think of gas as the fuel that runs Ethereum transactions and smart contracts - a bit like the gas used to fuel your car.

Gas units are actually just tiny bits of ether. The only difference is that miners can separate the gas price from the market price of ether. This way, if the ether price goes up, gas fees stay in check!

The future of Ethereum, Proof of Stake (PoS)?

Like Bitcoin, Ethereum mining currently uses lots of electricity. Soon, the Ethereum team plans to fix this by changing from PoW to **Proof of Stake (PoS)**. PoS doesn't have mining so it doesn't need much electricity. Since it's also faster to confirm transactions with PoS, the move could help Ethereum reach its full potential.

With PoS, there are **validators** instead of miners. Instead of solving complex cryptographic puzzles with their computers (like miners do) validators confirm transactions by **staking** their ether. A bit like with Dash masternodes from the last chapter, game theory incentivizes validators to correctly confirm transactions and secure the Ethereum blockchain.

The more ether a validator stakes, the higher chance he or she has of winning the total block reward. With PoS, that block reward is the total block transaction fees, rather than 5 new ether coins. This means new ethers would stop being created if Ethereum moves to PoS[4].

Proof of Stake (PoS)

Assume there are 5 validators for an Ethereum block. Each validator stakes ETH to stake a claim on the total transaction fee reward. As shown in the below diagram, validator 1 stakes 45% of the total ETH for the block. Validator 1 now has a 45% chance of winning the total block reward. Validator 2 has a 20% chance, validator 3 has 10% chance, and so on...

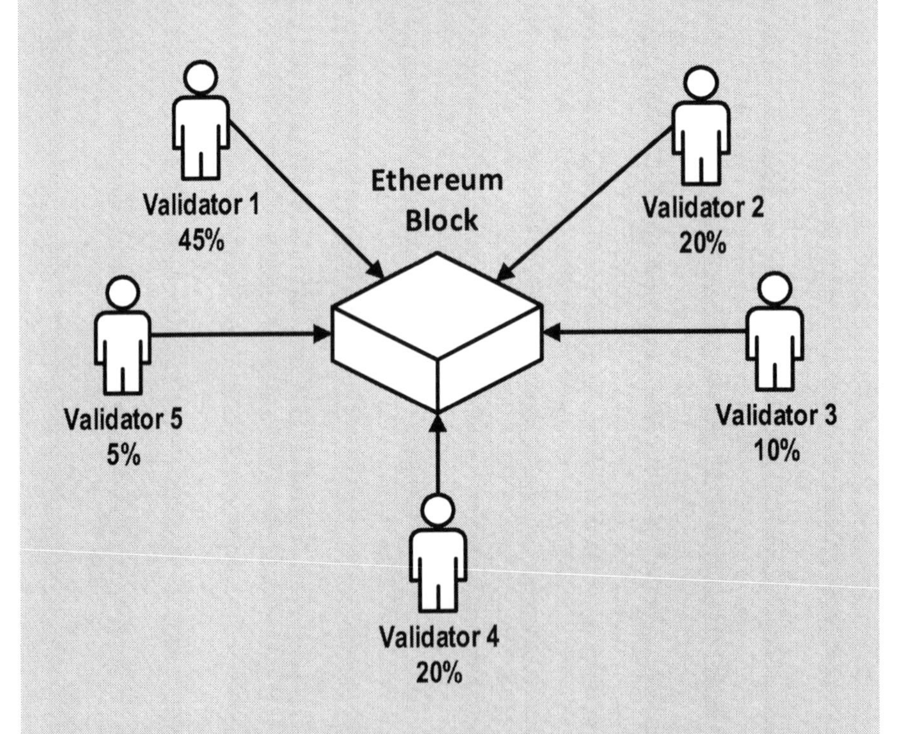

A random calculation, much like a wheel of fortune, then selects the winner. As fortune would have it, validator 3 (with a 10% stake) wins

[4] This is not always the case with PoS. Peercoin (PPC), for example, uses PoS to create new coins.

this time. Over many calculations, however, validator 1 would win 45% of the time given the probabilities shown from each stake in the previous diagram.

PoS could potentially make Ethereum easier to grow. There are three reasons for this:

1. **PoS is cheaper**: with PoW miners need to spend money on expensive mining equipment and electricity to get a return on their investment. There is no mining with PoS.

2. **PoS is faster**: it's faster for a validator to stake a claim with PoS than it is for a miner to mine a block with PoW.

3. **PoS has less risk of centralization**: the increasing expenses of PoW create barriers to entry for miners, which can make mining more centralized. Recall from chapter two that Bitmain China mines over 30% of the world's new bitcoins.

   With PoS, someone would need to own over 30% of all the ether in the world to have as much network power as Bitmain. You've got to be pretty rich for that, but stranger things have happened! To stop this, Vitalik and the Ethereum developers plan to launch **Casper**, a special PoS where validators lose their stake if they break the rules[32].

What happens next with Ethereum and PoS remains to be seen. Right now, PoS is still being developed and explored by the Ethereum team. As a crypto investor, this could be something to keep an eye on.

Decentralized Applications (dApps)

The Ethereum blockchain was designed so that developers can add new features to it if they like. These features are called **dApps**. DApps run on smart contracts and can be used for many different purposes. Ethereum dApps are powered by gas but often have their own **crypto tokens**.

The next page lists some examples of dApps being developed on the Ethereum blockchain...

- **Augur** is a decentralized prediction market platform. Users can bet on future outcomes with bitcoin and ether. They can bet on anything from London's weather tomorrow to Amazon's stock price next month. With lots of people betting on the same thing, there is consensus of the crowd. This makes Augur a powerful prediction tool.

  To make sure truthful outcomes are reported to Augur smart contracts, Augur has a system of **reporters** and **Reputation Tokens (REP)**. REP tokens are awarded to reporters who tell the truth and taken away from reporters who lie!

- **Alice.Si** is trying to incentivize charities to be more honest and efficient by holding funds for charity donations in Ethereum smart contracts. Per the website, Alice is a "platform that brings transparency to social funding through blockchain technology."[33] People can donate fiat currency (like pounds sterling) to charity goals that are programmed into smart contracts.

  Interactions by users within the Alice network require fee payments in **Alice Tokens**. This lends greater transparency to how charity organizations use fiat donations.

- **Ethlance** is a decentralized platform for freelance workers from all over the world to trade work for ether. Through Ethereum smart contracts, freelancers get paid as soon as the job is done. Unlike centralized freelance job platforms, Ethlance doesn't have service or membership fees. This is a great example of how blockchain can be used to cut out the middleman.

Checkout www.stateofthedapps.com to see the hundreds of different dApps that have already been built or are being built on the Ethereum blockchain.

Smart contracts and dApps are still in the very early stages of development so we don't yet know their true potential. We also don't know if Ethereum will still be the leading dApp platform in years to come.

Ethereum alternatives

Litecoin, Dash and Monero are all alternative cryptocurrencies to Bitcoin. After Ethereum, alternatives like Lisk, Stratis, Neo and Waves were born, which all allow developers to build their own dApps on top of them. This is a bit like Apple, Google and Microsoft all having their own app stores. Below are some examples of Ethereum alternatives which all use Proof of Stake (PoS):

- **Lisk (LSK)** allows developers to build dApps using the Microsoft Azure cloud computing platform.

- **Stratis (STRAT)** allows companies to easily build their own private or public blockchain-based applications on the Stratis platform.

- **Waves (WAVES)** lets its users launch their own custom cryptocurrencies on the Waves platform. It also offers decentralized trading and crowdfunding.

- **Neo (NEO)** has been dubbed the "Chinese Ethereum" with a strong focus towards regulatory compliance in China. Developers can build new smart contracts for all sorts of industries and applications on top of its blockchain.

- **Cardano (ADA)** has been dubbed the "Japanese Ethereum" - it plans to launch ATM's and debit cards in Japan[34] in 2018. Like Ethereum, Cardano is a programmable blockchain, where developers can program smart contracts and dApps to its blockchain.

The above list spells one word for investors: *diversification*. Ethereum may not be the most scalable technology right now, but its development team are working hard to change that. It also has a strong first mover advantage in the dApp arena.

That said, all the above cryptos (and many more not mentioned in this book) also have great teams of developers who are working tirelessly to improve their platforms.

The competition, therefore, is still wide open!

I've only written chapters on a handful of cryptos in this book. There are still two more chapters on this to come. If you would like to know more about other cryptos not mentioned in this book, I encourage you to research them further online. I've included some resources at the back to help with this. I will also be writing more about other cryptos on ***www.stopsaving.com****.*

Chapter Summary

1. *Ethereum takes blockchain technology to a whole new level. It's a programmable blockchain.*

2. *Developers can program smart contracts on the Ethereum blockchain. Smart contracts add 'if' conditions to payments. They could one day automate everything from financial derivative settlements to election voting.*

3. *Ethereum currently uses Proof of Work (PoW), which at the moment requires lots of electricity for mining and could potentially cause long-term scalability issues for its platform.*

4. *Ethereum plans to implement Casper, a type of Proof of Stake (PoS), where validators confirm and secure Ethereum transactions by staking ether. There would be no miners with this type of PoS and no new ethers would be created. PoS uses less electricity, is faster, and could be more decentralized than PoW.*

5. *DApps are apps without middlemen. They can be built on the Ethereum blockchain and run on smart contracts.*

6. *Some of Ethereum's competitors include Neo, Cardano, Stratis, Lisk and Waves. It's hard to say which platforms will lead the dApp space many years from now, so it makes sense for investors to diversify.*

CHAPTER 5

FORKS, BITCOIN CASH AND ETHEREUM CLASSIC

"If you see a fork in the road, take it"

Yogi Berra

It goes without saying that you should have a basic understanding of cryptos before investing in them. That said, there's a lot of jargon in this area. Knowing all the jargon is great if you want to write crypto code and start your own blockchain. But for the average crypto investor, jargon isn't that important.

Forks, however, are a bit of jargon that all crypto investors must understand.

What is a fork?

A **fork** is a change to a blockchain. The change can be temporary or permanent depending on the type of fork.

Temporary forks happen all the time with Bitcoin and other cryptos. You don't really need to worry about them as an investor. **Permanent forks** don't happen that often, but when they do, it's worth paying attention to what's going on.

Temporary forks

Temporary forks relate to transactions on the blockchain.

To understand temporary forks, think back to chapter two when you learnt about Bitcoin mining. Remember, new blocks are rewarded to the miner who solves the cryptographic puzzle. Once a miner solves the puzzle, the rest of the network quickly verifies the solution and the block of transactions is confirmed and added to the blockchain. It's easy for the network to verify the solution after a miner finds one.

Most often, one miner solves the puzzle. But sometimes, two miners solve the puzzle within split seconds of each other. At first, there is a temporary disagreement amongst the network on which solution to verify first. The disagreement is short-lived, however, as the network quickly agrees on a single solution and the next block is mined.

With temporary forks, there is a *temporary* disagreement amongst the network. But once the disagreement is resolved, everything goes on as normal!

Permanent forks

Permanent forks cause permanent changes to the rules of a crypto network. They happen every time something changes in the way Bitcoin, Ethereum or any other crypto works.

No fork, no change.

For example, if there's an upgrade to the Bitcoin protocol, there needs to be a change in the code, so a permanent fork must happen. After the fork, computers (nodes) on the Bitcoin network upgrade their software so that they can benefit from the system change.

There are two kinds of permanent forks: **soft forks** and **hard forks**. Here's an analogy to explain the difference between the two:

- An Apple iPhone software upgrade is like a **soft fork**. If you don't install the update, your phone still works. But if you do install the update, your phone works better than it did before. You have the choice to upgrade your phone's software or not. But given the advantages of upgrading (and the disadvantages if you don't), you end up installing the update eventually.

With cryptos, soft forks are a way to change the rules of the system gradually. In this case, the computers (nodes) on the network don't *need* to upgrade their software, but they end up doing it eventually because they are disadvantaged if they don't.

For example, a soft fork may give Tim, a miner, the option to upgrade his mining software. Tim can still mine coins if he doesn't upgrade, but he won't be able to mine new coins as effectively as the other miners who do upgrade. So, after some time, Tim upgrades!

To sum up, a soft fork is a gradual change to the network rules, which happens because network participants have the option (but also the incentive) to go with the new rules.

- **Hard forks** are more disruptive to blockchains than soft forks. In the Apple iPhone analogy, a hard fork would be like Apple releasing a new iPhone with a new feature, such as an improved camera, that doesn't exist on previous iPhone versions. If you want the improved camera, you need to buy the new iPhone!

You come to a fork in the road. You can either:

1. Buy the new iPhone with the new camera, or

2. Keep your old iPhone without the new camera.

With cryptos, hard forks can split the blockchain in two. Network participants can either stay on the old blockchain (with the old rules) or join the new blockchain (with the new rules). The diagram opposite shows what this looks like.

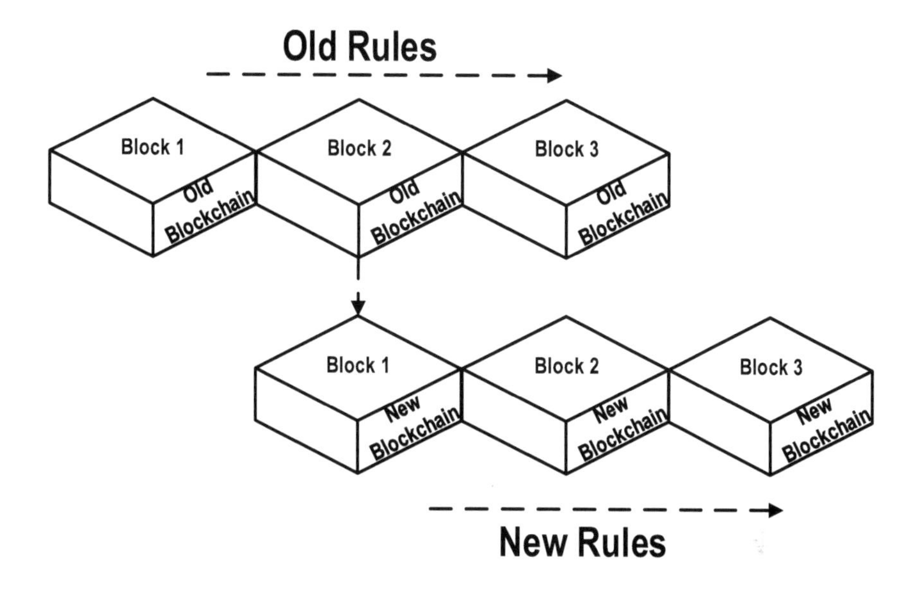

Hard forks can be either:

1. Unanimous, or

2. Contentious

1. Unanimous hard forks

Sometimes a crypto development team may wish to execute a hard fork that has already been planned in the project roadmap. This is usually a protocol upgrade of some kind that benefits the entire network. When this happens, network participants often unanimously agree to the network change and follow the new rules created by the hard fork.

If the whole network agrees the hard fork, there are no miners left to mine blocks on the old chain (before the protocol upgrade). The old chain, therefore, effectively stops working and a new chain is formed with new rules. This is shown on the diagram over the page.

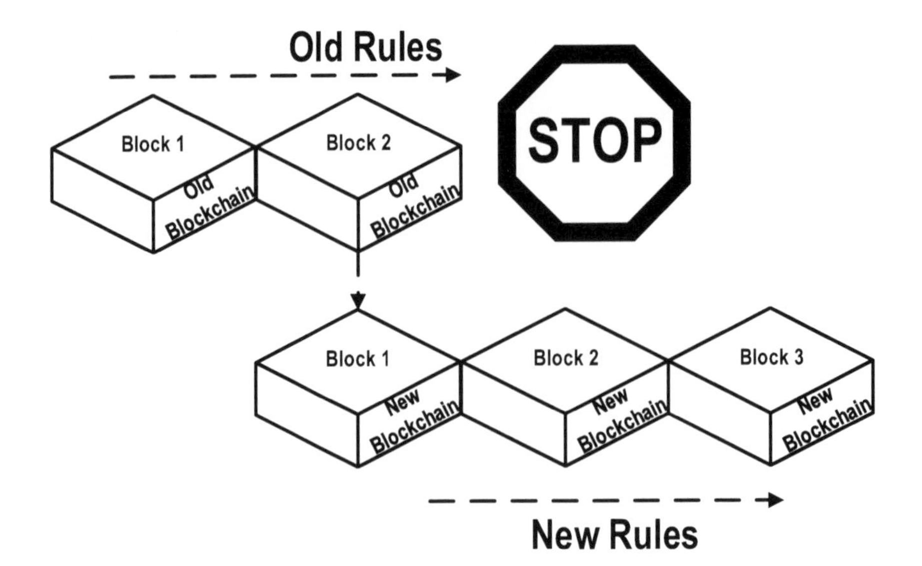

Unanimous hard forks are a part of life with cryptos. Think back to chapter three when you learnt about Monero using ***Ring Confidential Transactions (RingCT)*** *to mask how much money is spent in each transaction. RingCT wasn't a Monero feature at first. To upgrade Monero to have RingCT, the Monero team planned a hard fork for January 5th, 2017*[35]*.*

2. Contentious hard forks

The best way to explain these are through the examples of Bitcoin Cash and Ethereum Classic. In each case, the blockchains split in two, creating brand new cryptocurrencies. As explained over the next few pages, investors who paid attention to these forks received new crypto coins for free.

Bitcoin Cash:

On August 1st, 2017, Bitcoin hard forked into two separate blockchains: Bitcoin and **Bitcoin Cash (BCH)** [36].

There's a lot of politics in Bitcoin. Some people want one thing, others want another. **BCH** happened because of an argument over how Bitcoin should work, which had to do with the Bitcoin block size...

Satoshi originally coded Bitcoin to have a 1MB block size limit. This means blocks can store up to 1 MB worth of transaction data, which isn't a lot of storage. So, if too many BTC transactions happen in the same block, some of them must be included in later blocks. This is why we sometimes have bitcoin transaction backlogs.

The demand for block space has resulted in people paying higher transaction fees to miners so they can jump the queue. This is good for miners, who secure the blockchain, but bad for people making bitcoin payments.

With this dilemma, one part of the Bitcoin network (miners) wanted to stay on the smaller 1 MB block size, the other wanted to increase the block size (Bitcoin users).

To cut a long story short, BTC hard forked to create BCH. We now have BTC still with a 1 MB block size, and BCH with an 8 MB block size[37].

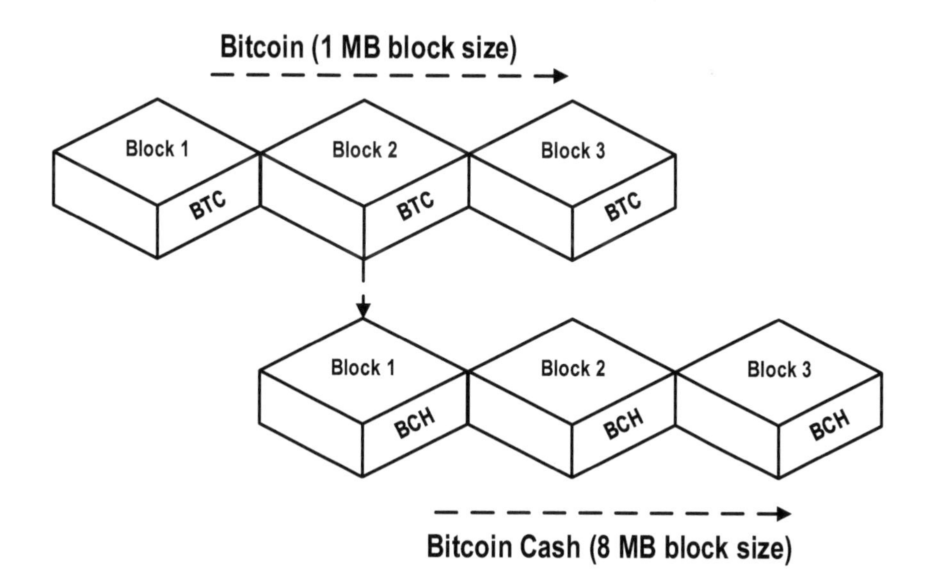

Since we are dealing with cryptocurrencies, there were, of course, a few other technical things going on that caused the fork. One of these was **Segwit**.

A closer look at Segwit

Segwit is another piece of jargon you may want to understand. It stands for **Segregated Witness.**

Recall from chapter two that each Bitcoin block is split into two parts:

1. Block Header.
2. Block Body.

The **block header** has all the things needed for the PoW hashing algorithm to run, such as the hash of the last block, the difficulty target, the nonce and so on. Remember for PoW miners try to solve puzzles to get new bitcoins.

The **block body** has all the transaction data. This includes the details of the sender and the receiver as well as a **digital signature** for each transaction. The digital signature proves that the sender has enough bitcoins to send the receiver.

Since digital signatures are long cryptographic pieces of code, they take up a lot of storage space for each transaction.

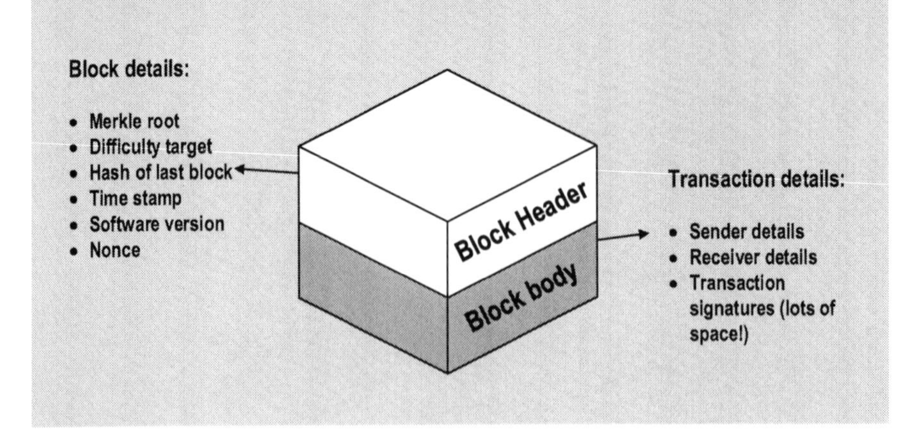

To get around the problem of digital signatures taking up too much block space, Bitcoin core developer Pieter Wuille came up with Segwit[38]. The basic idea behind Segwit was to optimize the transaction signature data to free up more block pace.

This was a brilliant solution to increase Bitcoin's transaction capacity, but it came with another problem:

Since Segwit would be a huge change to the Bitcoin system, the developers origionally built it so that 95% of the network must approve it[39]. This would have been difficult for the network to agree:

- On the one hand, more free space in the blocks would mean more transactions could go in them, leading to lower transaction costs. This would benefit bitcoin senders and receivers.

- On the other, lower transaction fees would give miners less incentive to mine bitcoins. Mining is essential to the security of Bitcoin.

This predicament caused delays in the activation of Segwit and concerns over the potential health of the Bitcoin network. So, the developers compromised: a **Segwit soft fork** was activated on August 23rd, 2017. Now, network users could choose to either:

1. Upgrade their Bitcoin software and use Segwit, or

2. Not upgrade and keep going on as normal.

While debates about Segwit raged on, Bitmain proposed the **Bitcoin Cash hard fork** as a contingency plan to the Segwit soft fork[40]. Unlike Segwit, the hard fork didn't originally need a 95% network majority to be approved - people in the network could either choose Bitcoin or Bitcoin Cash.

The Bitcoin Cash hard fork then occurred on August 1st, 2017, almost a month before the Segwit soft fork was activated. Unlike Bitcoin, Bitcoin Cash does not have Segwit.

What about the Bitcoin investors?

Investors who owned BTC at the time of the hard fork received equal amounts of BCH. On August 2nd, one BCH coin was worth 0.2465 bitcoins[41]. Investors who sold BCH at this time would have locked in a 25% return - without selling any of their original bitcoins.

Those who never sold, however, now own another coin that may (or may not) keep rising in value with time.

Ethereum Classic and the DAO hard fork

In the last chapter, you learnt that developers can build decentralized Apps (dApps) on the Ethereum blockchain. One of these dApps was Ethereum's version of the **Decentralized Autonomous Organization (DAO).**

The DAO was a decentralized investment company that would collect and manage funds raised to build dApps on the Ethereum platform. It would use a voting process to choose which dApps got funded.

This seemed like a good idea at the time and investors got pretty excited. The DAO **Initial Coin Offering** (we discuss 'ICOs' in detail in chapter twenty) raised over $160 million in ether from 10,000 unknown investors to fund the project[42]. At the time, this was the largest amount of money ever raised in an ICO.

But then in June 2016, soon after DAO coins started trading on major crypto exchanges, an unknown hacker found a loophole in the coding of the DAO dApp. This allowed the hacker to steal one-third of the total ethers raised in the ICO. At the time, that was worth over $50 million.

The Ethereum developers came to a fork in the road. They could either:

1. Re-work the Ethereum code and return the stolen ethers to their rightful owners, or

2. Accept the issue and move on.

Vitalik, his key developers, and most of the Ethereum network went with the first choice. But some people thought otherwise. They believed that re-working the code went against the ethos of Ethereum smart contracts, which were meant to be *unchangeable*.

This disagreement caused a hard fork of the Ethereum blockchain. Ethereum was split into:

1. **Ethereum (ETH)**: where the code was re-worked, and

2. **Ethereum Classic (ETC)**: where nothing was done.

Many investors (but not all) see Ethereum as the better long-term investment because it kept Vitalik and the key developers. Any updates or improvements to Ethereum - such as the Proof-of-Stake upgrade described earlier in the last chapter - won't automatically apply to Ethereum Classic.

As was the case with Bitcoin Cash, investors who owned ether at the time of the fork received an equal amount of **Ethereum Classic (ETC)** coins. Again, some investors got 'free money' from this.

In conclusion

With blockchains, forks are a fact of life, but they aren't always a bad thing. However, they can cause uncertainty for investors. Even if you own the original coins, there are no guarantees you will receive the new ones. You'll learn how to potentially profit from future forks in part two of this book. But in the next chapter, let's explore a cryptocurrency that doesn't use blockchain at all...

1. *For a cryptocurrency system to change how it works, it needs to fork its blockchain. There are various kinds of forks.*

2. *Temporary forks happen when two miners mine the same block at the same time, or in quick succession. The network quickly agrees on the solution of one miner and everything goes on as normal.*

3. *A soft fork is a gradual change to the network rules which happens because network participants have an incentive to go with the flow.*

4. *A hard fork can split the blockchain in two. Network participants can either stay on the old blockchain (with the old rules) or join the new blockchain (with the new rules).*

5. *The whole network agrees unanimous hard forks. This can happen when a development team plans a hard fork to upgrade the protocol of a crypto. The plan is usually stated in the project roadmap.*

6. *Other hard forks are contentious. This happens when the network disagrees how a cryptocurrency should work. That's how Bitcoin Cash and Ethereum Classic were created.*

7. *Sometimes hard forks create brand new cryptocurrencies, or 'free money' for the holders of the original coins.*

CHAPTER 6

IOTA AND THE MACHINE ECONOMY

"IOTA's seemingly 'out of nowhere' explosive growth can be traced back to the fact that it has been somewhat of a sleeping giant".

David Sønstebø

So far, the cryptos we've covered use chains of transaction blocks to achieve consensus-based decentralization. IOTA takes a different approach to cutting out the middleman: the **tangle**.

IOTA and the tangle

IOTA was developed in 2015 by David Sønstebø, Sergey Ivancheglo, Dominik Schiener and Dr Serguei Popov[43]. On IOTA's website (iota.org) the tangle is described as the "next generation blockchain". Like blockchain, the tangle is a decentralized system that verifies transactions using cryptography. But unlike the blockchain, the tangle has:

- No blocks.
- No transaction costs.
- No miners competing to mine new coins.

To recap, with blockchain:

1. Each transaction goes into a block.

2. Miners solve cryptographic puzzles to mine blocks of transactions.

3. Once a miner finds a solution to the block, the rest of the network verifies that solution. This confirms the block of transactions on the blockchain.

4. Each block after that adds more layers of confirmation to all the blocks before it (and the transactions within each block).

Instead of being a chain of blocks (blockchain), the tangle is a **web of interconnected transactions**. Each *transaction* uses **Proof of Work (PoW)** to confirm two earlier transactions before it. This PoW is a lighter version of the Bitcoin PoW because:

- **It needs less hashing power to solve**: any desktop, laptop, or smartphone can solve the puzzle.

- **It uses much less electricity** because ordinary home computer and mobile devices are the **nodes** that perform PoW.

As more transactions occur on the IOTA network, more transactions are confirmed, and each transaction is confirmed to a greater degree. So just like with blockchain, the more transactions, the more secure the network becomes.

How does the tangle work?

The tangle is a type of **Directed Acyclic Graph (DAG).**

Transactions in the tangle are called **states.** Each state is connected to a node on the IOTA network. A transaction cannot be made until a node solves the PoW and confirms two transactions that came before it. The diagram on the next page shows what this looks like:

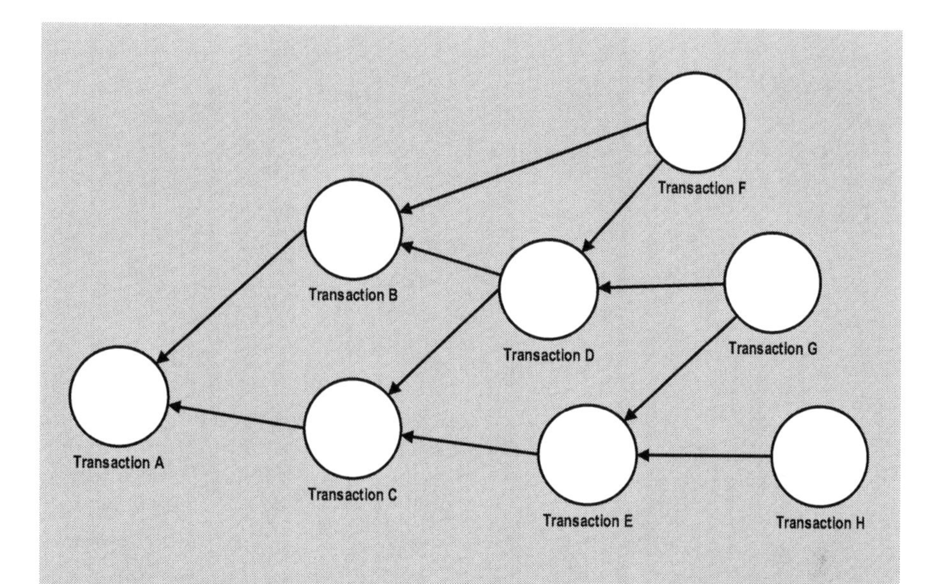

As shown above:

- Transaction A (state A) is the most buried in the tangle out of all the transactions. Transaction A is, therefore, the most secured.

- Transactions F, G and H are all new transactions (called **tips**). These are **unconfirmed transactions** in the tangle.

  Tips can only join the tangle once they have confirmed two transactions before them. Transaction F, for example, only joins the tangle once it confirms transactions B and D.

IOTA and iota tokens (IOT)

IOTA is the tangle system that confirms and processes all **iota token** transactions.

IOTA aims to solve some of the problems currently associated with Bitcoin:

- **Scalability**: recall from the last chapter that Bitcoin can only process a set number of transactions per block. If there are too many transactions happening at once, they can't all fit in the next block. This competition for block space (supply and demand) can drive up transaction fees.

As mentioned in chapter two, Bitcoin can currently only process between three and four transactions per second[44]. Bitcoin developers are working on speeding this up with solutions such as **Lightning Network**, but IOTA can already process up to 1,500 transactions per second with no fees[45]. Unlike Bitcoin, IOTA gets faster as more transactions occur on its network. This means IOTA's transaction speed could go up in the future as its network use grows.

- **Centralization:** Bitcoin is decentralized but competition amongst miners has caused high mining costs, which have in turn raised barriers to entry for miners. Recall from chapter two how Bitmain, for example, controls a significant part of the Bitcoin network through the BTC.com and AntPool mining farms.

The pie chart below from blockchain.info shows the hashing power distribution rate for Bitcoin at the time of writing[46].

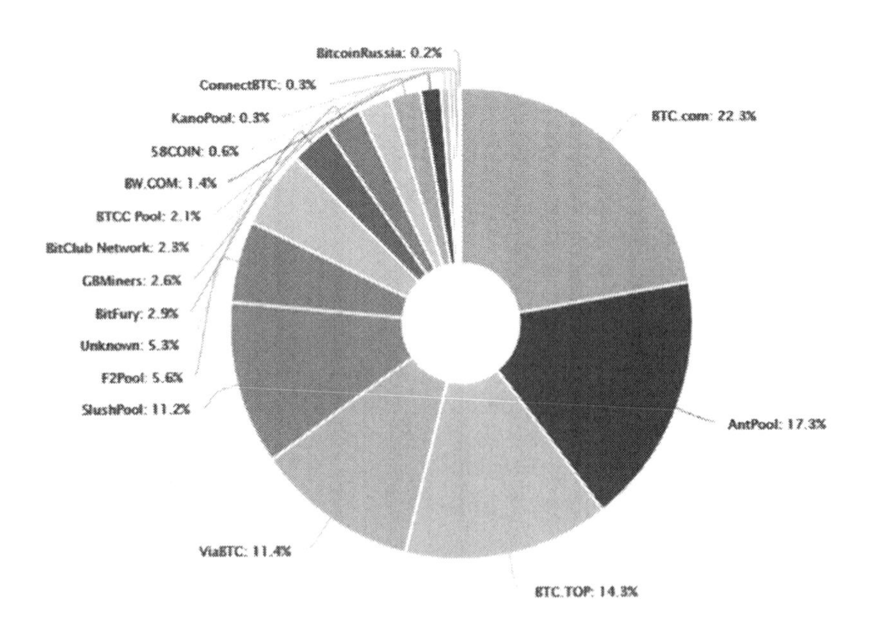

IOTA has its own PoW but it doesn't have miners who compete to secure the network in exchange for financial rewards. Therefore, IOTA doesn't have the potential problem of competition amongst miners leading to centralized mining pools.

IOTA and the internet of things

The **internet of things (IoT)** is a system where various electronic 'things' exchange information online. As a simple example, you wake up in the morning to your alarm clock. Your alarm clock then sends a signal to turn your kettle on for your morning cup of tea.

In the IoT, most devices would have their own IP (Internet Protocol) address. The IOTA network could then allow these IP addresses to interact with each other through smart contracts built on its platform.

IOTA would also allow these devices, with their own IP addresses, to make and process transactions - this is why some people believe IOTA will one day become the platform that powers the machine economy.

The future of IOTA

The concept of IOTA and the tangle looks great on paper. But like other cryptocurrencies, IOTA's technology is still in the very early stages of development. For IOTA to become the platform for the internet of things (IoT), it needs the IoT to become a reality. We're still a long way off from that!

IOTA's tangle becomes more secure as more people use it. Right now, it needs a lot more people using it before it can compete with the security of blockchain. This is something to keep an eye on in the future.

Byetball

Like IOTA, Byteball is a cryptocurrency that uses a Directed Acyclic Graph (DAG), rather than a blockchain, to run its network.

Byteball is a decentralized database. Instead of having states in its DAG (like IOTA does), Byetball has **storage units**, which can securely store and exchange financial value or digital data.

Byetball tokens, called **GBYTES**, buy storage space on the database. One GBYTE buys one gigabyte of storage pace.

To finish up part two...

With new cryptos joining the market every week, investors will be presented with more opportunities, and more problems, as they try to navigate this new and exciting market.

That's the end of part one of this book. I hope you now know what cryptos are and have a basic understanding of how they work. If you want to learn more about the different coins available, checkout the back of this book for more resources.

Up next in part two, you'll learn a potential system for investing in cryptos from start to finish!

1. *IOTA doesn't use blockchain. It uses the tangle.*
2. *The tangle has no fees, no miners and no blocks.*
3. *Instead, the tangle is an interconnected web of transactions. Each transaction verifies two transactions before it.*
4. *The deeper a transaction is 'tangled in the tangle', the more secure it becomes.*
5. *IOTA uses a lighter PoW than Bitcoin. You can solve IOTA's PoW on your mobile phone (you don't need an expensive mining rig). When your toaster gets its own IP address, you might be able to use that too.*
6. *Unless something better comes along, IOTA could be the ideal platform to power the Machine Economy (or internet of things) in the future.*

PART 2: INVESTING IN CRYPTOS WITH THE CRYPTO PORTFOLIO

CHAPTER 7

INTRODUCING THE CRYPTO PORTFOLIO STRATEGY

"He who lives by the crystal ball is destined to eat ground glass."

Ray Dalio

The investment returns of cryptocurrencies have so far been astronomical. One bitcoin was worth five cents in July 2010[47]. On December 17th, 2017, it reached $20,000 for the first time. That's a 39,999,900% return on investment. Put another way, the value of bitcoin increased 400,000 times in just over seven years. Not too shabby.

And if that's not enough to make you second guess some of your recent life decisions, have a look at the price changes over 2017 for some of the other coins you read about in part one of this book:

Coin	Price Jan 1st 2017	Price Dec 31st 2017	% Return on investment	Growth of $100 invested
Litecoin	4.51	232.10	5,046%	$5,146
Ripple	0.0064	2.30	36,018%	$36,118
Monero	13.97	349.03	2,398%	$2,498
Dash	11.23	1051.70	9,265%	$9,365
Ethereum	8.17	756.73	9,162%	$9,262
Neo	0.14184	75.96	53,453%	$53,553
Lisk	0.15025	20.41	13,484%	$13,584
Stratis	0.07238	14.03	19,284%	$19,384
Waves	0.22132	12.60	5,593%	$5,693

FOMO (fear of missing out)

With these FOMO-inducing returns, it's easy to get carried away. But nothing lasts forever, especially when it comes to investing. Sooner or later, the music must stop. And those who invested too much too late in the game could find themselves in a world of financial pain.

But here's the thing. We don't know if the music will stop tomorrow, or if the main act is yet to take the stage. It's impossible to predict the future of any financial market, especially cryptos, which have only been around for a few years. One thing we do know, however, is that enormous risks lie ahead.

Risks can be good or bad depending on how you invest.

Once we accept that we *don't* know what will happen with cryptos tomorrow, we can then begin to form an investment strategy. This is what we'll cover in this part of the book.

Why invest in cryptos?

Before we get started with the strategy, here are some quick reasons why you may wish to consider investing in cryptos:

1. If you follow a good investment strategy, you can potentially make some money.

2. You can take part in the growth and adoption of new technologies that promote a decentralized and fairer economy.

3. You can invest in cryptos with very small amounts of money - you don't need to risk it all.

4. Crypto returns don't usually depend on whether the stock market goes up or down (for now anyway), so they can help diversify (and therefore reduce the risk) of your overall investment portfolio. In other words, owning digital assets might actually *protect* you in a global financial crisis or stock market crash (assuming you also own stocks).

5. There are plenty of free online resources to improve your understanding of cryptos (see the resources section at the back of this book). There's a lot to learn up front, but it will all 'click' soon enough. After reading part one of this book, you already know more about cryptos than most people.

Introducing the Crypto Portfolio

In part one of this book, you learnt what cryptos are and how they work. Now, you're ready to learn how to invest in them using the **Crypto Portfolio (CP)** investment strategy. A CP is your own investment fund made up of ten different crypto coins.

The CP aims to:

1. Reduce the risks of investing in cryptos as much as possible.

2. Earn steady investment returns from cryptos over time.

3. Limit the time you spend investing in cryptos, so you can get on with your life!

Let's break each of the above aims down in a bit more detail...

CP Aim 1: reduce investment risk

Investing in cryptos can be financially rewarding, but it's also risky. With the CP strategy, you'll try to reduce these risks as much as possible.

To that end, we'll focus on:

1. Choosing crypto investments with long-term growth potential.

2. Diversification - not putting all your eggs in one basket.

3. Investing small amounts of money consistently, rather than going all-in when you think there's a good buying opportunity.

4. Keeping your coins safe from thieves (hackers) by using good exchanges and wallet storage methods.

5. Taking your emotions out of your investment decisions. Emotions can cause investors to make costly mistakes.

CP Aim 2: earn steady returns over time

This aim links up well with CP aim 1 above.

In crypto chat forums, people talk about the *moon* a lot. Here's what I have to say about that:

The journey to the moon is long. While trying to take shortcuts may seem like the faster route at first, it's also the more dangerous. People see the huge returns made from bitcoin and other cryptocurrencies in the past, so they often take unneeded risks trying to get rich quick.

For example, they might see the price of an unknown crypto token rocketing up, so they invest more money into it than they can afford to, *hoping* the price will go up by much more.

Trying to get rich quick will doom you from the start. Slow and steady usually wins the race.

Remember, if you lose 50% of your money, you need to make 100% to get back to where you started. The CP strategy aims to limit large losses as far as possible and let the power of compounded investment returns take care of the rest.

CP Aim 3: spend less time in front of your trading screen

Crypto exchanges don't sleep. Unlike the stock market, they're open seven days a week, twenty-four hours a day. If you want to keep your stress levels down, spending your days and nights with one eye on the crypto market won't help you.

We all have jobs, hobbies, families, friends, people to see and places to go. Investing should give you better life, not consume it. Investing should be as stress-free as possible, automated and profitable over time!

Let's get stuck in

It will take some time at first to get your CP up and running. For starters, you need to finish reading this book. But once you understand the process, investing is highly automated. With the CP strategy, you only buy or sell cryptos once a month.

Over the next several chapters, we'll cover what you need to know!

Chapter Summary

1. *Crypto investing is risky. You need a strategy to help reduce the risks of investing in them as much as possible.*

2. *FOMO is not an investment strategy.*

3. *The Crypto Portfolio strategy aims to:*

    - *Reduce the risks of investing in cryptos.*
    - *Earn steady returns over time, rather than try to make quick profits.*
    - *Reduce the time you spend investing in cryptos, so you can get on with more important things in life.*

CHAPTER 7

DON'T INVEST TOO MUCH IN CRYPTOS

"The four most dangerous words in investing are: 'this time it's different'"

Sir John Templeton

As you invest more money in risky investments, the risks go up - and cryptos are as risky as they come! And yet the more money you invest, the more profit you could potentially make over time. How much should *you* invest? Conventional financial wisdom suggests you base this decision on two things:

1. Your **ability** to take risk: how much risk can you afford to take?

2. Your **willingness** to take risk: how much risk would you like to take?

1. Ability to take risk

I'm sure you've heard the saying "only invest what you can afford to lose". With crypto investing, you should take this literally. The higher your ability to take risk, the more money you can afford to invest in cryptos, or the more money you can afford to lose if things go wrong.

You have a higher ability to take risk if you:

1. **Earn a steady and secure income.** This can be through a monthly paycheck, your own business, or a skillset that allows you to earn money when you need to. In other words, you don't rely on investment income to pay your bills.

2. **Already have a diversified investment portfolio**. If you own other investments like stocks, bonds, gold, mutual funds, or buy-to-let property, then you are in a good position to add cryptocurrencies to the mix. The returns of cryptos are uncorrelated (don't depend on) the returns of other assets, so they could help diversify your overall investment portfolio. This could mean less risk overall.

   Later in this chapter, we'll cover more on why it's good to own other assets besides cryptos.

3. **Have more years of investing left ahead of you**. As with all investments, crypto returns go up *and* down in the short term. The longer you plan to invest for, the more time your investments have to recover from the bad times.

4. **Have little or no debt.** If you are in a lot of debt, then it's best to pay it off before you start investing. This will, of course, depend on the size of the debt compared to your income and the interest rate on the debt.

   If, for example, you take out a £5,000 loan with a yearly interest rate of 15%, then you need to make at least 15% return on your investments each year to break even.

Having a mortgage on your home also counts as debt. Make sure you never invest money you've put aside for this!

5. **Don't have big and important expenses coming up.** If you need to make a down payment on a house, wedding reception, engagement ring or college tuition for you or your children, then set that money aside. Don't put it in cryptos!

To sum up the above points, ask yourself how much spare change you could afford to invest. To help with this, draw up a budget spreadsheet to take stock of where you are financially.

2. Willingness to take risk

If you have spare change to invest, you can then decide how much of that you *want* to invest in cryptos. Do you prefer taking risks or playing it safe? Only you can know the answer to this.

When making this decision, don't just think of the risks of investing but think of the risks of *not* investing too. Fortunately, we all get to retire someday. Unfortunately, government pensions aren't what they used to be. When you retire, you'll need income from your investments (crypto or otherwise) to comfortably see out your twilight years.

Mixing cryptos with other assets: diversification

In the book *Cryptoassets: The Innovative Investor's Guide to Bitcoin and Beyond*, Chris Burniske and Jack Tatar refer to bitcoin as the "silver bullet of diversification" [48].

Cryptos are a new asset class. Their returns don't usually move with the returns of other investments like stocks or bonds. As explained in the below example. this makes cryptos good for diversification.

The benefits of mixing cryptos with other assets

In this simple example, assume:

- Joe invests £1,000 in cryptos at the start of the year.
- 'Steady Eddy' invests £100 in the same cryptos as Joe and invests the other £900 in stocks.

One year later, cryptos have dropped by 40%. Since he had all his money in cryptos, Joe loses £400.

Steady Eddy, on the other hand, also owns stocks, which went up 10% during the year. This means Eddy:

- Only **loses £40** (40% x £100) on his cryptos.

- **Gains £90** (10% X £900) on his stocks.

Eddy's total return for the year is **£50** (£90 gain on stocks - £40 loss on cryptos). Eddy does much better than Joe because he diversified into other investments besides cryptos.

The above example shows what would happen if cryptos went down. Diversification would also help if the stock market went down and cryptos went up. The point is, don't put all your eggs in one basket.

Spread your risks and you will be rewarded over time. Not just financially, but with better sleep too!

What portion of your investment portfolio should go into cryptos?

With risky investments you can earn or lose lots of money. With 'safe' investments your upside isn't as high, but you have less chance of large losses. Diversifying your investments by splitting them between riskier and safer assets is a great way to build wealth over time - without taking too much risk overall.

Since cryptos are extremely risky, they should only take up a small part of your portfolio. Here's why:

- Crypto returns can be huge. A small investment could give a big boost to your portfolio.

- On the flip side, crypto losses can be huge too. Having too much invested could cause a serious dent in your wealth if things go wrong in the crypto market.

The next example looks at this further:

Joe cuts back on his crypto exposure

Joe learnt a lot from his mate 'Steady Eddy' last year. He now speaks to a financial adviser who suggests he put 5% of his money in cryptocurrencies, 10% in gold and the other 85% in mutual funds[5]. The mutual funds are made up of lots of different stocks, so they're well diversified.

Joe has £10,000 to invest so he puts:

- £500 in cryptos.
- £1,000 in gold.
- £8,500 in mutual funds.

This year, the crypto market booms. Joe's investments in Litecoin, Ethereum and Monero have altogether earned him over **£2,000** in profit. His gold, however, went down 10%, losing him **£100**. But he made a 10% return (or **£850**) on his mutual funds.

The table below shows the changes to Joe's portfolio during the year:

Investment	Value at start of the year	Value at end of the year	Profit or loss
Cryptos	£500	£2,500	£2,000
Gold	£1,000	£900	-£100
Mutual funds	£8,500	£9,350	£850
Total	**£10,000**	**£12,750**	**£2,750**

As shown above, Joe made a big difference to his overall investment return by having just a small amount of his wealth in cryptos.

Overall, Joe's total portfolio returned **£2,750** for the year (or 27.5%). This is a brilliant return for Joe considering he didn't need to take so much risk to achieve it.

[5] This is specific to Joe in this example and is not a recommendation as an ideal portfolio split.

As a worst-case crypto scenario, the table below shows what would have happened if Joe lost the whole £500 he invested in cryptos for the year:

Investment	Value at start of the year	Value at end of the year	Profit or loss
Cryptos	£500	£0	-£500
Gold	£1,000	£900	-£100
Mutual funds	£8,500	£9,350	£850
Total	**£10,000**	**£10,250**	**£250**

Even in the worst-case scenario for cryptos, Joe's portfolio still didn't lose him money overall. In fact, he made a small profit. By only investing 5% of his wealth in cryptos, Joe limits his potential crypto losses to a small part of his total portfolio.

There's always the chance Joe's mutual funds could also go down. Even if that happened, Joe would still have limited his losses from cryptos to £500. This is because Joe only owns £500 worth of cryptos at the start of the year. A small loss is always better than a large one!

Mutual funds are a great way to diversify your investments as they are made up of lots of different stocks. To learn more about mutual funds, read my other book 'Stop Saving Start Investing: Ten Simple Rules for Effectively Investing in Funds'.

Rebalancing

The last example shows the benefits of splitting your portfolio into different types of assets. Riskier assets like cryptocurrencies should take up a smaller percentage of your total wealth than safer investments like diversified mutual funds, for example.

But what happens when those percentages change over the year? **Rebalancing** is a simple way to restore order to your investment portfolio.

Rebalancing: Joe cuts back on his cryptos again

Another year has gone by and Joe is a wiser investor for it. Recall from the last example, Joe's investment portfolio grew 27.5% last year, from £10,000 to £12,750:

Investment	Value at start of last year	Value now	Profit or loss
Cryptos	£500	£2,500	£2,000
Gold	£1,000	£900	-£100
Mutual funds	£8,500	£9,350	£850
Total	**£10,000**	**£12,750**	**£2,750**

Because cryptos did so well last year, they now take up a much larger chunk of Joe's portfolio. Remember, Joe started with 5% in cryptos, 10% in gold and 85% in mutual funds. But here's what his portfolio split looks like now:

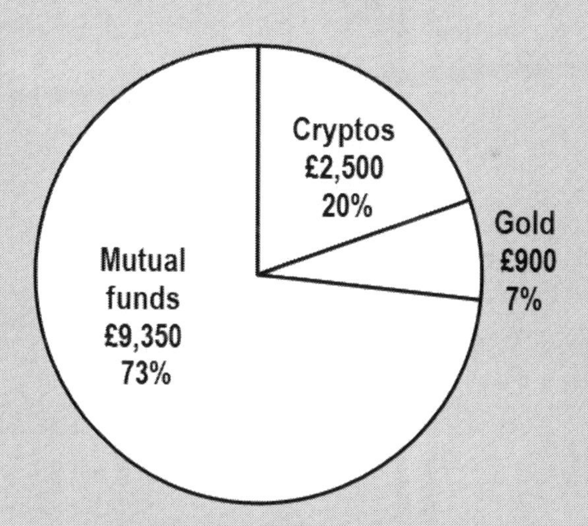

This makes Joe uncomfortable. He's got too much of his wealth invested in cryptos!

Joe now wants to restore his portfolio back to its original percentages just in case cryptos do badly this year:

Investment	Value now	Value at 5,10 and 85% splits	Difference
Cryptos	£2,500	£637.50	-£1,862.50
Gold	£900	£1,275	£375
Mutual funds	£9,350	£10,837.50	£1,487.50
Total	**£12,750**	**£12,750**	**£0.00**

To get his portfolio back to its original 5,10 and 85% split, Joe:

1. Sells **£1,862.50** of cryptos.
2. Uses that money to buy **£375** of gold and **£1,487.50** of mutual funds.

With rebalancing, you sell stuff that's expensive (has gone up in price) and buy stuff that's cheap (has gone down in price). You buy low and sell high. Over time, this can improve your investment returns and lower your risks.

As it turns out, the next year was terrible for cryptos. They lost 90%!

If Joe had not rebalanced, he would have lost **£2,250** (90% of £2,500). But because he rebalanced, he only lost **£573.75** (90% of £637.50).

Rebalancing seems to be working well for Joe. So much so, that Eddy now regularly asks him for help!

To sum up...

Only invest a very small part of your total investment portfolio in cryptocurrencies. Find a portfolio split that suits your investment goals and level of risk. If that split changes over the year, rebalance it. Once a year is enough.

More active investors might rebalance once a quarter, once a month, or even once a week. One of the advantages of rebalancing more often is that you could lower your risks in very volatile market conditions. At the same time, more frequent rebalancing leads to higher trading costs and could lower your overall returns if one of your assets is in a strong bull market for the year.

Hopefully, you're now closer to deciding how much money you want to invest (if any) in cryptos. Do some more research after reading this book to see what works for you. If you're still unsure after that, you may want to ask a financial adviser who understands cryptos for help.

For the rest of this book, we'll focus on how to potentially improve the returns and reduce the risks of crypto investing.

We will start this journey in the next chapter by digging deeper into the **Crypto Portfolio** strategy.

Chapter Summary

1. *How much you invest in cryptos should depend on two things:*
    - *Your ability to take risk.*
    - *Your willingness to take risk.*
2. *You have a high ability to take risk if you can lose most of your investments in a year and still be OK financially.*
3. *You have a high willingness to take risk if you enjoy taking risk when investing.*
4. *Build an investment portfolio with a few different asset types. Only invest a small part of it in cryptos. Find a percentage portfolio split that works for you.*
5. *Once a year, rebalance your portfolio to restore it back to its original split. This forces you to buy low and sell high. Rebalancing means:*
    - *Buying more of the assets that went down over the year.*
    - *Selling some of the assets that went up over the year.*
6. *If you don't rebalance, you could end up with too much money invested in risky (and expensive) assets at the end of the year. This means you could potentially lose more money next year.*

CHAPTER 8

HOW TO CHOOSE COINS

"Know what you own, and know why you own it."

Peter Lynch

If you're going to invest in cryptos, try investing in good ones. For the Crypto Portfolio (CP) strategy, you choose ten different crypto coins. I'll explain why ten is a good number in the next chapter. But for now, let's focus on the coins themselves.

As I write this, there are over 1,100 different coins to choose from. Since this number keeps going up, choosing the right coins can be hard work. In this chapter, let's try to make these choices easier for you.

What makes a coin a potentially good investment?

A coin is worth considering for the CP strategy if it:

1. Has a **good development team**, with lots of interest from other developers.

2. Has a **strong crypto community** who believe in it.

3. **Solves a real problem** in the world using crypto technology.

4. Has a large **market capitalization**, meaning the market already likes it.

5. Has high **liquidity** on exchanges.

Let's now look at each of these in more detail...

1. Core Development Team and developer interest

Just like companies need good management teams, cryptos need good **development teams**. Good development teams have great technical skills and high integrity, and they genuinely want their coin to do well. To that end, they're always looking for ways to improve the technology behind their crypto projects.

Here are some examples of this:

- The Ethereum core developers plan to move Ethereum from Proof of Work (PoW) to Proof of Stake (PoS) to make it more scalable.

- The Dash development team are trying to make dash payments more user-friendly through the Dash Evolution payment system.

- The Monero team made Monero transactions more private with Ring Confidential Transactions (Ring CT).

There are many more examples like those above, but I think you get the point. These are all things to keep an eye on when choosing different coins for your CP. You can do this by visiting the websites of each crypto (just google the name, it usually ends with a ".org") and looking at the development team and **development roadmaps**.

Development teams can be made up of miracle workers but without **money to pay their expenses**, it's hard for them to stay on top. There are many ways for development teams to get funding. Dash, for example, has the *Decentralized Autonomous Organization (DAO)*. Ethereum has the *Ethereum Foundation*. Bitcoin has many sponsors funding its developers to keep improving its tech.

Crypto websites often show how the team is funded. If they don't, Google will show this. If that doesn't do it, the team is most likely working on goodwill.

Cryptos are **open-source**. This means other developers (not part of the core team) can work on the code. If there's a lot of outside developer interest, that's often a good sign for the future of a coin.

Later in this chapter, you'll learn a straightforward way to tell if developer interest is high.

2. *Crypto community behind the coin*

News spreads fast in the age of social media. It could be promising if lots of people are talking about a cryptocurrency on Facebook or Reddit.

When looking online for public interest levels, you want consistent discussions over time. If people on social media are praising a coin one week and ridiculing it the next, it could just be short-term hype. Just like football teams, good coins need strong communities of loyal supporters to get them through the tough times!

As mentioned in chapter two, Bitcoin was the second most searched word in Google in the *Global News* category in 2017. This most definitely had something to do with its rise to over $20,000 per coin in December that year. According to a study by SEMrush, the price of Bitcoin has a 91% correlation to the number of google searches for Bitcoin or Bitcoin-related terms[49].

The reason for this is simple: the more interest in something, the more people want to buy it.

Towards the end of this chapter, you'll learn how to easily check the community support levels of any cryptocurrency.

3. Does the coin solve a unique problem?

What problem is the coin trying to solve? How big a problem is it? Does the coin offer a good solution to that problem using *crypto* technology?

Here are some examples of cryptos that solve problems:

- Bitcoin helps people bank without a bank account. This has enormous potential when you think that billions of people around the world don't have bank accounts. Because of Bitcoin's strong security and finite supply, it also serves as 'digital gold': a secure way to store value without the need for a trusted middleman.

- Litecoin and Dash can currently process transactions faster than Bitcoin with lower fees, so they could be better for smaller transactions than Bitcoin.

- The Ripple system helps banks move value quickly and cheaply to one another. It's better than the current banking payment system, SWIFT, which is expensive and takes days to process international transactions.

- Monero, Dash and Zcash all have their own ways of making financial transactions more private. This could help people in third world countries keep their money out of reach of corrupt governments. It could also help corporations keep sensitive financial information secure.

- Ethereum, Neo, Waves, Stratis, Cardano and Lisk are all platforms for smart contracts and dApps.

- Iota offers a means of crypto payment to operate the machine economy via the tangle.

4. Market Cap

The **market cap** of a crypto is the total amount of money invested in it at any point in time. The below equation calculates it:

Market Cap = Current Coin Price x Current Coin Supply

The **current supply** is the total amount of coins available at a point in time. The current supply of bitcoin, for example, is just under 17 million bitcoins. This is the total amount of bitcoins that have been mined so far. In 2140, once all the bitcoins have been mined, the current supply will be 21 million bitcoins.

A high market cap can be a sign of investor confidence. It means lots of investment has already gone into a cryptocurrency. It also usually means more people are buying and selling the coins, so it's often good for liquidity too (we'll discuss this shortly).

In the case of cryptos, it could be wise investing in coins that are at least in the top twenty or thirty by market cap. These coins already have a stamp of approval from other investors.

Always compare market caps in the same currency. At the time of writing, below are the top ten coins by market cap as shown on coinmarketcap.com:

Top ten coins by market cap (source: coinmarketcap.com)

Rank	Name	Market Cap	Price	Current Supply
1	Bitcoin	$257,957,868,518	$15,373.20	16,779,712 BTC
2	Ripple	$112,222,266,533	$2.90	38,739,144,847 XRP
3	Ethereum	$86,525,500,908	$894.35	96,747,017 ETH
4	Bitcoin Cash	$46,497,397,835	$2,752.72	16,891,438 BCH
5	Cardano	$27,638,775,735	$1.07	25,927,070,538 ADA
6	Stellar lumens	$15,411,862,742	$0.862096	17,877,200,152 XLM
7	Litecoin	$13,754,985,390	$251.93	54,598,008 LTC
8	NEM	$12,682,079,999	$1.41	8,999,999,999 XEM
9	IOTA	$11,209,762,245	$4.03	2,779,530,283 MIOTA
10	Dash	$9,094,614,599	$1,166.56	7,796,097 DASH

Market cap

The Market cap of a coin depends on both its **price** and **supply**. Since different cryptos have different supplies, market caps are a way to compare apples to apples.

Let's now compare the market caps of Bitcoin (BTC) and Ripple (XRP) to explain this further.

Looking at the table of data from coinmarketcap.com:

Rank	Name	Market Cap	Price	Current Supply
1	Bitcoin	$257,957,868,518	$15,373.20	16,779,712 BTC
2	Ripple	$112,222,266,533	$2.90	38,739,144,847 XRP

People new to crypto investing might look at Ripple and think "if BTC's price is over $15,000, then maybe XRP could also be $15,000 one day."

This statement doesn't factor in the different coin supplies of XRP and BTC. If XRP were $15,000 a coin, its market cap would be over half a quadrillion dollars![6] This is because the supply of XRP is over 2,000 times higher than that of BTC.

A better statement would be:

"Based on my research, I think Ripple has the potential to one day have a larger market cap than Bitcoin. Looking at the numbers, if the price of BTC stays roughly the same, the XRP price would have to rise to about $7 a coin for that to happen."

The box above shows that market cap is more important than price when choosing crypto investments. This is because market cap factors in price *and* supply.

As a separate point, market cap is also a factor when assessing the threat of *crypto whales*...

---

[6] To put that into perspective, the entire global derivatives market is estimated to have a notional value of $1.2 quadrillion. Source: https://moneymorning.com/2013/09/18/heres-what-1-2-quadrillion-looks-like/.

Whales, market cap and 'pump and dump'

Whales are crypto investors who can afford to own large chunks of a coin's total market cap. Some whales use their power and wealth to bully the smaller fish.

An example of this is a **pump and dump.** Here, whales team up with each other to put in large buy orders, quickly pumping up the price of a coin. The unsuspecting fish see this as the start of a rally, so they buy some coins for themselves. This drives the price up even more.

Once the price is high enough, the whales quickly dump their positions by selling their coins at large profits. This leaves the fish in murky waters.

Most of the time, the smaller the market cap, the easier it is for a few whales to own most of the coins, so the easier it is for them to pump and dump.

Jordan Belfort from The Wolf of Wallstreet movie was a pump and dump master in the late 1980s and early 1990s with small cap stocks. But the regulators got him in the end. With time, the crypto market will become more regulated; this will be the crypto whale's harpoon!

For the CP strategy, you invest in larger market cap cryptos to try and keep risks down. Larger market cap cryptos are usually more liquid (see the next page), and more established investments than smaller cap ones – of course, there are always exceptions.

As a side note, you can make a lot of money investing in smaller cap cryptos if you know how. But the risks go up. More on that in part three of this book.

5. Liquidity

A coin is **liquid** if people are buying and selling it often. Good liquidity means:

- **Lower spreads**: since more buyers and sellers are matched, the price at which you buy and sell a coin is closer together.

- **Easier exits**: if you can't sell your coins because nobody wants to buy them, that's bad. You could end up selling them for less than you bargained for.

- **More investor interest**: if people are buying and selling a coin all the time, that means traders like it. Just like high market caps, good liquidity can be another stamp of approval from the market.

- **Harder to pump and dump**: if there are more people trading a coin, it's harder for whales to team up together. Smaller cap coins are often less liquid than larger cap ones, so they're easier targets for *whale cartels*.

Three methods to choose coins

Making a checklist of the above points is a great approach to choosing your coins. The more research and analysis you do, the better.

I'll now go over three methods that can make choosing coins easier:

1. The Market cap method

Remember how a high market cap and a good level of liquidity can be stamps of approval from other investors? Since high market caps and high liquidity often go hand in hand, choosing ten coins with the highest market caps seems sensible.

For the CP strategy, you invest 10% of your crypto wealth in each of your ten coins. In the next chapter, I'll explain why ten is a good number.

Coins with the highest market caps often have the right ingredients. They wouldn't have so much invested in them if they didn't. The cream usually rises to the top in the stock market, so why should cryptos be any different?

To use the **Market cap method**, go to www.coinmarketcap.com or www.cryptocompare.com/coins/list and choose the top ten coins. Invest 10% of your CP in each coin.

It's worth noting that there is a difference between how Coinmarketcap and CryptoCompare calculate the market cap:

- Coinmarketcap's method includes all coins owned by ordinary investors as well as coins owned by the developers, founders and team members behind the crypto.
- CryptoCompare's method only includes coins owned by ordinary investors, so the market cap is said to be 'free floating'.

All crypto investments are risky. This includes large caps! If you want to take more risk in search of higher returns, you can invest in small cap cryptos. But be warned, small caps are typically more volatile than large caps, meaning they move up and down more quickly and by larger amounts. The CP strategy aims to keep risks down and make steady returns over time.

2. The coingecko.com method

Coingecko.com ranks coins by a rating system based on three criteria:

1. **Developer rating**: this tracks online public source code archives to see how much interest and effort there is from developers. The

higher the developer rating, the more work is being done to improve the coin.

2. **Community rating**: this tracks the level of interest from the online crypto community by looking at feeds from Facebook, Reddit and various crypto forums. A strong community interest contributes to more trading and investing.

3. **Public interest rating**: this tracks search engine results and overall web popularity. Popular cryptos tend to go up in price over time.

For each coin, Coingecko takes an average of the above three ratings to get an overall rating. The next table shows the ratings of the top ten coins on Coingecko at the time of writing:

Rank	Name	Developer rating	Community rating	Public interest rating	Total rating
1	Bitcoin	98%	87%	52%	91%
2	Ethereum	93%	72%	42%	83%
3	Ripple	81%	77%	36%	82%
4	Stellar Lumens	85%	63%	34%	75%
5	Litecoin	74%	70%	38%	74%
6	Verge	83%	67%	36%	74%
7	Cardano	86%	59%	32%	74%
8	Monero	89%	62%	38%	73%
9	Neo	84%	64%	38%	73%
10	IOTA	77%	66%	42%	72%

To use the **Coingecko.com method**, go to coingecko.com and choose the top ten coins. Invest 10% of your CP in each coin.

3. The Gecko-Market cap combo method

If you can't decide between the Market cap or Coingecko method, you can combine them. To do this, you could use the below ranking system:

1. On a spreadsheet or a piece of paper, make two columns. One for Market cap coins and another for Coingecko coins.

2. In each column, if a coin is ranked number 1, it gets a score of 1. If it's ranked number 2, it gets a score of 2...and so on.

3. Enter the rankings in the 'Market cap rank' column for the first fifteen coins (you may need to do more than this depending on the rankings).

4. Then enter the 'Coingecko rank' for each coin next to it...

Coin	Market cap rank	Coingecko rank	Total score
Bitcoin	1	1	2
Ripple	2	3	5
Ethereum	3	2	5
Bitcoin Cash	4	12	16
Cardano	5	7	12
Stellar lumens	6	4	10
Litecoin	7	5	12
NEM	8	26	34
IOTA	9	10	19
Dash	10	13	23
Monero	11	8	19
Neo	12	9	21
Eos	13	11	24
Tron	14	40	54
Bitcoin Gold	15	72	87

5. For each coin, add the numbers from each column to get the total scores.

6. Then rank the totals from smallest to largest, as shown on the next page...

Coin	Market cap rank	Coingecko rank	Total rank
Bitcoin	1	1	2
Ripple	2	3	5
Ethereum	3	2	5
Stellar lumens	6	4	10
Cardano	5	7	12
Litecoin	7	5	12
Bitcoin Cash	4	12	16
IOTA	9	10	19
Monero	11	8	19
Neo	12	9	21

7. Finally, choose the top ten coins for your Crypto Portfolio. Invest 10% of your CP in each coin.

The Market cap, Coingecko and Gecko-Market cap combo methods can all help automate the process of choosing your cryptos.

These methods help filter out coins that haven't yet proven themselves to investors, developers, the crypto community and the public. You can use any of the three methods to either:

1. Choose which coins you want to invest in, or

2. Do a **first screening** of the coins available to narrow your choices down. Here, you can filter to the top twenty or thirty coins in each method. Next, you can do some more research online to see which coins you want to buy. This combination of automation and doing your own research could prove highly effective.

Since the crypto market changes by the second, the top ten coins for each method also changes over time. In chapter ten, we'll look at why it could be a good idea to keep owning the same coins for at least a year.

Up next...

There are lots of cryptos to choose from, but hopefully, this chapter makes things easier. In the next chapter, we'll look at diversification in more detail and explore the potential benefits of choosing ten different coins for your CP.

Chapter Summary

1. *For the CP strategy, choose ten coins that:*

    - *Have good development teams.*
    - *Have strong community and public support.*
    - *Solve real problems.*
    - *Have large market caps.*
    - *Have high liquidity on exchanges.*

2. *The market cap of a coin equals its current price multiplied by its current supply. It helps you make apples to apples comparisons between different coins at a point in time.*

3. *The Market cap, Coingecko, and Gecko-Market cap combo methods can all help you choose ten coins for your CP, or at least narrow your choices down.*

4. *If you want to take your investing further, there are no substitutes for doing your own research before choosing each coin. The more research you do, the better off you'll be.*

CHAPTER 9

TEN COINS ARE BETTER THAN ONE

"Don't look for the needle in the haystack.
Just buy the haystack."

John C. Bogle

In the last chapter, you learnt how to choose coins for your CP. Now, we'll focus on why it's important to spread your bets through diversification.

A quick history of dot com stocks

If the recent history of the stock market teaches us anything, it's that picking the winners is not easy. There are two main reasons for this:

1. Existing companies are always competing for market share.

2. New and disruptive companies can come out of nowhere and take market share.

In 1996, around 80% of the world used *Netscape* internet browsers to surf the web[50]. On August 9th, 1995, Netscape became a public company by floating its shares on the Nasdaq through an **Initial Public Offering (IPO)**. On its first day of trading on the Nasdaq, the Netscape share price more than doubled - it started the day at $28 per share and ended it at $58.25 per share.

The company still hadn't made a cent in profit. But at the time, many investors betted that it would one day become the biggest internet company the world had ever known. And when the Netscape share price finished that year at 174 bucks a share, many of them thought they had betted right.

At about the same time this was going on, a guy named Larry Page met another guy named Sergey Brin at Stanford University[51]. Working out of their dorm rooms, they built a search engine called *Backrub* that could rank web pages on the World Wide Web. They decided Backrub wasn't such a great name, so they changed it to *Google* instead. It wasn't until August 19th, 2004 that Google shares started trading on the NASDAQ, almost a decade after Netscape's IPO.

The internet gave birth to many great companies, but it was the likes of Google, Amazon and Facebook that did the best as long-term investments. It was impossible for anyone to know this in 1995, just as it's impossible for anyone to know in 2018 which cryptos will one day rule the world. Bitcoin may have most of the market share right now, but so did Netscape in 1996.

The chart below from coinmarketcap.com shows how the market shares of some of the largest cryptocurrencies have changed over 2017. Nobody knows what this chart will look like one year from now, let alone in the next five to ten years.

Total market dominance percentages (coinmarketcap.com)

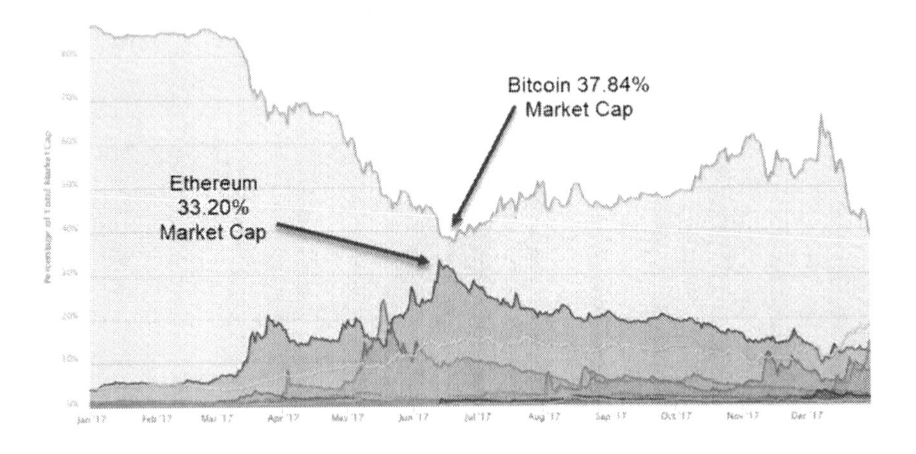

There's a lot going on in the previous chart, but let's focus on Bitcoin and Ethereum to keep things simple. Bitcoin started the year with just under 90% of the crypto market share, but by June 19th its market share had dropped to only 37.84%. Ethereum started the year with a market share of less than 5% but peaked for the year on June 13th with a market share of 33.20%. Within days of each other, Ethereum's market share nearly took over Bitcoin's.

But for most of the second half of the year, Bitcoin's market share went up again, as Ethereum's drifted down.

Investors who owned both Bitcoin and Ethereum last year would have spread their risk without having to predict which coin would dominate the market at the end of the year.

Why it makes sense to diversify

Through **diversification**, you spread your investment risk by owning more than one investment. The more coins you own, the more diversified you are, and the less dependent your returns are on the performance of a single crypto investment.

Diversification lowers the **volatility** (how much investments go up and down) of your CP. Here's a simple hypothetical example:

A quick diversification recap...

- Allesandro owns 1 coin. During the week, it drops 60% after a fork goes wrong.
- Lucia owns 10 coins, including the one Allesandro owns.

Over the same week, each of Lucia's coins makes different returns. Some go up, some go down. Overall, Lucia is much better off than Allesandro.

Another benefit of diversification is that it can help protect you from yourself. Your crypto wealth is less likely to have large swings in value when it's diversified, so you are less likely to let your emotions get in the way of your investment choices.

When investors get emotional they often make bad calls. One example of this is **panic selling** - selling investments after a huge price crash fearing what might come next.

Even if you are diversified, your CP can still have huge drops in value in a single day. Sometimes all cryptos go down together, which reduces the benefits of diversification. In crypto, 10 - 20% daily market drops are part of the deal!

Why the number ten?

In the last chapter we covered some methods for choosing ten coins for your CP. But why ten? Why not twenty or thirty?

There are three reasons for this:

1. Just like SPF for sunscreen, diversification has **diminishing power**. Each time you add a new investment to your portfolio, you make it more diversified. But keeping all other factors constant:

    - The first ten coins add most of the potential diversification benefits - they reduce your portfolio risk by the most.

    - The next ten coins only add marginal diversification benefits - they reduce your risk by less.

    - The next ten coins only reduce your risk by a tiny amount.

2. Having more than ten coins is **hard to manage**. The CP strategy is supposed to be simple and not take up a lot of time. If you have more than ten coins, you will spend more time:

    - Making trades each month.
    - Choosing cryptos.
    - Sending coins between different exchanges (covered in chapter fourteen).
    - Monitoring the performance of all your different cryptos (covered in chapter seventeen).

3. If you have more than ten coins, you **spread your investments too thinly**. Unless are already rich, you won't be able to put enough money into each investment to capitalize on the potential gains if one of them goes 'to the moon'.

    Although cryptos are risky investments, some coins can go up over 1,000% in a year. Let's face it, the potential for such massive returns is what makes cryptos so appealing to many investors. Having ten different coins is a good middle ground between:

    1. Having enough money invested in each coin to profit if one of them goes up massively, and
    2. Getting enough diversification benefits.

Digging deeper into the CP diversification strategy

It would be sensible to invest 10% of your CP in each of your ten coins. This way, you don't have too much invested in each one. These percentages will change each month as the returns for each coin go up or down, so rebalancing is key. We'll get to that in the next chapter.

Cryptos can be grouped into various categories. For example:

1. **Regular cryptocurrencies** like Bitcoin and Litecoin.

2. **Privacy cryptocurrencies** like Monero, Zcash and Dash.

3. **Smart contract crypto platforms** like Ethereum, Neo and Stratis, each with their own coins to power the network.

4. **DAG cryptocurrencies** like IOTA or Byetball.

5. **Tokens** or **appcoins** for dApps. For example:

    - **Steem** uses Smart Media Tokens to pay users of the social media platform Steemit.com for writing content.

    - **Golem** is a worldwide open-sourced supercomputer where users can earn Golem Network Tokens by renting out their computing power for building and selling software.

At the time of writing, there aren't any tokens or appcoins in the coinmarketcap.com or coingecko.com top ten. Today, dApps tend to be younger and riskier investments than the other categories mentioned above, so there's less reason to include them in your CP.

Saying that, most of the new crypto coins coming to the market every week are dApp tokens, so this is an area to keep an eye on. We'll look at ways to potentially invest in dApps and other smaller market cap cryptos in the advanced section at the back of this book.

Excluding dApp tokens for the reasons explained above, you can diversify your CP so that it is spread out amongst the above categories.

Final thoughts on diversification...

Diversifying your crypto investments is a great way to reduce the risks of your Crypto Portfolio. But it's only part of the story. As mentioned earlier, sometimes all coins go down together, so diversification alone won't help you.

In the next chapter, we'll look at another way to reduce the risks of your crypto investments. It works well by itself, and even better with diversification...

1. *Diversification means your investment returns don't depend too much on the performance of a single investment. You don't put all your eggs into one basket.*

2. *Like SPF for sunscreen, diversification has diminishing power as you add more cryptos to your portfolio.*

3. *For the CP strategy, you invest in ten different coins. This still gives you most of the diversification benefits without making your life difficult.*

4. *When choosing ten coins for your CP, make sure you diversify into different types of cryptos. Some categories include:*

    - *'Regular cryptocurrencies'*
    - *Privacy cryptocurrencies*
    - *dApp platforms*
    - *Tangle cryptos*

5. *DApp tokens tend to be smaller cap cryptos, so they don't fit into the CP strategy. Checkout part three of this book for more on investing in smaller cap cryptos.*

6. *You want 10% of your CP invested in each of your ten cryptos. This way, you don't have too much invested in one coin, but you have enough invested in each for your CP to profit if one of them 'moons'.*

CHAPTER 10

DON'T INVEST TOO MUCH IN ONE GO

"Buy cheap and sell dear"

Benjamin Graham

Cryptos go up and down like yo-yos. So if you invest lots of money into them all in one go, you could be in trouble if prices crash just after you invest. As with most investments, it's safer to invest small amounts of money over time than a large amount all at once.

Dollar Cost Averaging (DCA)

DCA is a simple process where you invest the same amount of money each month. Over time, this averages the prices at which you buy your coins.

Say you want to invest $1,200 in *Coin X*. Instead of investing the whole amount at once, you invest $100 each month for twelve months in a row.

- If the price goes down after your first $100 investment, you may be disappointed. But, you would now get a better bargain in month 2.

- If the price goes up instead, you would happy you got in cheap. But in month 2, you would now have to spend the same amount of money, $100, to buy fewer coins than you did in month 1.

Why the CP Strategy does NOT use DCA

In crypto slang, *HODL* means hold your coins. As in don't sell them...ever.

But with cryptos, you need to take some profits (by selling some coins) at the right times to protect you from the potential danger of losing most of what you invested. We have no idea where the crypto market will go next. It could keep going up for the years to come. Or, it could crash by 90% tomorrow.

DCA is an effective way to average the prices at which you buy your coins. But it doesn't tell you when to sell, or how much to sell. For this reason, we will not be using it for the CP strategy.

Instead, we will use...

Value Averaging (VA)

With Dollar Cost Averaging (DCA), you invest the same amount of money each month, regardless of how high or low the prices are.

With **Value Averaging (VA)**, you also invest small amounts of money each month, but the amounts differ depending on the price of the investment at the start of the month.

- If a coin does well one month, its price goes up, so you buy fewer of them.
- If it does badly the next month, its price goes down, so you double down and buy more of them at the lower price.
- If the price then goes up massively the next month, you sell some coins at a higher price. You take profits.

In other words, VA forces you to buy low and sell high because you:

1. Buy more coins when they're cheap (at good value).
2. Buy fewer coins when they're expensive (at worse value).

3. Sell coins when they're very expensive (at terrible value).

The below example explains how VA works in more detail. It's got a fair amount of maths, but it will make sense if you go over it a few times. It's important you fully understand how this strategy works before you consider using it.

How Value Averaging (VA) works

Bob wants to invest in *Coin X* using the VA strategy.

He wants to:

1. Invest a maximum of $1,200 of his own money into Coin X over the year.

2. Spread his purchases over the 12 months so that the *value* of his investment goes up by $100 each month.

   In other words, Bob wants to own:

   - $100 Worth of coins at the start of month 1.

   - $200 Worth of coins at the start of month 2.

   - $300 At the start of month 3...and so on...

   - Until he finally has $1,200 worth of coins at the start of month 12.

Each month, the total value of Bob's coins will be higher or lower than what he wants it to be according to his VA strategy, so he will buy or sell the difference to make it right.

Month 1 (start of investment, price doesn't matter)

- On the first day of month 1, Coin X costs **$10**.
- Bob wants to own $100 worth of coins at the start of month 1, so he **buys 10 coins** for $10 each.

The price of the coin makes no difference when starting the VA strategy. If it costs $1 or $1,000, Bob still invests $100. With cryptos you can usually buy coins in tiny fractions.

Month 2 (price has gone down):

- On the first day of month 2, Coin X costs **$5**.
- Since the coin price halved over the last month, the total value of the 10 coins Bob bought in month 1 has also halved from $100 to **$50**.

Remember that he wants the value of his investment to go up by $100 each month. This means he wants his investment to be worth $200 at the start of month 2.

But since his investment is now only worth $50, Bob must double down and invest $150 to get his value up to $200.

That's the bad news for Bob.

The good news is that Coin X is half as cheap as it was last month. It's only 5 bucks a coin!

At this price, Bob **buys 30 coins** for his $150. He now has 40 coins in total:

- 10 Coins he bought in month 1 at $10 each, plus
- 30 Coins he bought in month 2 at $5 each.

The average price at which Bob bought the coins over months 1 and 2 drops after he buys the 30 cheaper coins in month 2. So far, he's spent $250 altogether.

Bob's $250 spending is made up of:

- $100 He invested in month 1, and
- $150 He invested in month 2.

This means the average price Bob paid per coin is **$6.25** ($250 divided by 40 coins).

If Bob were instead using a simple DCA strategy, his coins would have been more expensive on average. Below is some maths to explain why:

1. *In the case of DCA, Bob would have spent $100 each month.*
2. *At $10 a coin in month 1, he would have bought 10 coins for $100.*
3. *Then in month 2, the price went down to $5 a coin. Bob would still spend $100, so he would buy 20 coins in month 2.*
4. *Over months 1 and 2, he would, therefore, have bought a total of 30 coins for $200. This would give Bob an average purchase price of* ***$6.67*** *per coin.*
5. *With VA (as explained above) he got a better bargain because he bought 40 coins at $6.25 each.*

Month 3 (price has gone up by a lot):

- By the first day of month 3, Coin X has bounced back up to **$10**.
- Bob's 40 coins, therefore, are now worth **$400**.

- Since he only needs to own $300 worth of coins at the start of month 3, he must now **sell $100** worth of coins.

Bob started the month with 40 coins. After he **sells 10 coins** at $10 each (or $100 worth of coins), he now has:

- 30 Coins, plus

- $100 in the bank from the sale.

Recall that before month 3, Bob had only spent $250. Now, he has sold $100 worth of coins.

- His *net investmen*t is, therefore, **$150** ($250 - $100) and he still owns **$300** worth of Coin X.

- Therefore, even though the price is the same as it was in month 1 ($10), Bob has doubled his return.

As shown in this example, VA works well with volatile investments. Cryptos are extremely volatile, so they're well suited to VA.

Month 4 (price goes up, but not by a lot):

- On the first day of month 4, 1 Coin X is **$12**.

- At $12 each, Bob's 30 coins (after he sold 10 coins last month) have now gone up in value from $300 to **$360**.

- Since Bob wants a $400 value invested at the start of month 4, he now only needs to **spend $40** ($400 - $360). For $40 he **buys 3.33 coins** (at $12 per coin).

- He now **owns 33.33 coins** in total (30 coins he had already plus 3.33 coins he bought in month 4) that are worth $400.

- So far, Bob has only spent **$190** in total ($150 net spending from month 3 plus $40 spending in month 4) for **$400** worth of coins, so he's still going strong!

VA with yearly spending cap:

What happens if Bob's $1,200 runs out before the year is up?

Suppose that after month 5, the price of Coin X keeps going down each month until the end of the year. With VA, Bob would invest more money each month the as the price goes down. This means he would end up investing more than $1,200 in total over the year.

If Bob had a high threshold for risk, this wouldn't be a problem for him. But since Bob is a more cautious crypto investor, he sets $1,200 as the *maximum* he would invest in Coin X for the year.

Suppose, for example, that:

1. By month 10, Bob's $1,200 runs out, so he stops investing.

2. In month 11, if the value is more than $1,100, he can then sell the difference and potentially use that money to buy more coins in month 12.

What about next year after the 12 months is up?

- Next year, Bob can keep holding Coin X and take profits every now and again (if there are in fact profits).

- He can then use those profits to invest in other cryptos, or other assets like stocks or bonds to diversify his overall investment portfolio.

VA and rebalancing your CP

In chapter seven you learnt why **rebalancing** between different asset types is a good idea. With rebalancing, you restore your portfolio back to its original percentage split after some investments do better than others. This way, you don't end up with too much invested in one asset, so you keep your risks down.

Rebalancing is a way to keep the right split between your different investments like cryptos, mutual funds and gold. But it's also good to rebalance *within* your CP to protect you from having too much invested in one coin.

As I'll explain in the below paragraph, VA does this for you each month as you always restore your CP to its original split of 10% in each of your ten coins.

Treating each coin in your CP separately is the easiest way to use VA. For example, if you were to use a £200 per month VA strategy, the value of each of your coins would go up by £20 each month. This way, you would rebalance your CP to 10% in each coin at the start of each month.

As part of my research for this book, I started a six-month VA portfolio on September 1st, 2017. I published the strategy to my blog: www.stopsaving.com/blog/my-crypto-investing-strategy.

In the article, I explain how I use a VA spreadsheet I built to invest in ten different cryptos. You can download the spreadsheet for free by following the link within the article. This will make VA much easier and more automated should you choose to use the strategy.

In this chapter, you learned how VA works. Up next, we'll put VA to the test...

1. *Investing large sums of money into cryptos all in one go is a bad idea; you could end up losing a lot of it if you invest just before a market crash.*

2. *It's much better to invest your money in small chunks throughout the year. This way you average the prices at which you by your coins.*

3. *Dollar Cost Averaging (DCA) is when you invest the same amount of money each month, regardless of what the prices of your crypto investments are doing.*

4. *The problem with DCA is that it doesn't tell you when to sell. Since cryptos are volatile, you need to take profits sometimes. For this reason, Value Averaging (VA) is used instead of DCA for the CP strategy.*

5. *VA is when you decide in advance how much you want the value of a crypto investment to go up by each month. You buy more or less, or sell coins to keep the value of your investment going up by the same amount each month.*

6. *For the CP strategy, use VA for each of your ten coins. VA rebalances your CP once a month to protect you from having too much invested in one coin. This is because at the start of each month you always have 10% invested in each crypto.*

CHAPTER 11

PUTTING VA TO THE TEST

"Past performance is not indicative of future results"

Securities Exchange Commission rule 156

In the last chapter, you became a certified VA maths expert and learnt how to use VA in your CP. Now let's see how VA would have performed in the past with Bitcoin, Litecoin, Ripple, Dash and Ethereum. I've used these coins because they've been around the longest, so there are more past prices to test the strategy.

Here are the assumptions and key points for the test:

1. Just like in the example with Bob in the last chapter, we assume a VA strategy of $1,200 value per year – or value increases of $100 each month for twelve months in a row.

2. To test the strategy, we are comparing VA with DCA and HODL (hold) investing.

    - **For DCA**, assume $100 is invested each month, totalling $1,200 over 12 months. Coins are never sold.

    - **For HODL**, assume $1,200 is invested on January 1st each year. As with DCA, coins are never sold with HODL.

I've included the results in various tables throughout this chapter. All the prices shown in the tables came from coinmarketcap.com, apart from the January, February, March and April prices for 2013, which came from quandl.com[52]. I built a spreadsheet in Excel to model the results.

VA past performance: Bitcoin

Over the next few pages, we'll use the assumptions described earlier to compare bitcoin's performance with VA to that of DCA and HODL from 2013 until the end of 2017. For each year, I've included a table showing the trades made in each month for VA. The bottom half of each table then shows a summary of the results for the year.

We'll begin with bitcoin in 2013. There are detailed explanations over the page of how I got the numbers in the table below. I'll give less detail for the remaining years, but the same logic applies.

VA Performance 2013 (Bitcoin)

Date	$ Bitcoin price	$ Starting monthly value	$ Value needed each month	$ Invested (+) or received (-)	No. bitcoins bought (+) or sold (-)
Jan 1st	13.22	0.00	100	100.00	7.5643
Feb 1st	20.35	153.93	200	46.07	2.2637
Mar 1st	34.55	339.56	300	-39.56	-1.1449
Apr 1st	104.70	909.12	400	-509.12	-4.8626
May 1st	116.99	446.95	500	53.05	0.4534
Jun 1st	129.30	552.61	600	47.39	0.3665
Jul 1st	88.05	408.58	700	291.42	3.3097
Aug 1st	104.00	826.80	800	-26.80	-0.2577
Sep 1st	138.34	1,064.15	900	-164.15	-1.1866
Oct 1st	132.18	859.92	1,000	140.08	1.0597
Nov 1st	206.18	1,559.84	1,100	-459.84	-2.2303
Dec 1st	955.85	5,099.60	1,200	-3,899.60	-4.0797
		Coins owned Dec 31		1.2554	
		Year-end price (Dec 31)		$754.01	
		Year-end coin value		$946.60	
		Net money invested		-$4,421.08	
		Average price per coin		-$3521.57	
		VA % annual return		**unlimited**	
		DCA % annual return		1,290%	
		HODL % annual return		5,603%	

Before we analyze the results for 2013, let's start with a quick refresher of **Value Averaging (VA)** as applied to the numbers shown in the table on the last page:

1. On January 1st, the bitcoin price was **$13.22**. The price didn't matter here as it was the first time VA was used. Therefore, you would have **spent $100** to get **7.5643 bitcoins**. This is shown at the top of the last column.

2. By February 1st, the bitcoin price went up to **$20.35**. Here's what would have happened with VA:

   - On February 1st, you would need a $200 value invested in bitcoin.

   - Since the bitcoin price went up over January, the value of your 7.5643 bitcoins bought in January went up too – they would now be worth **$153.93** at a price of $20.35 per coin.

   - To get to the value of your investment to $200, therefore, you would need to **spend $46.07,** which would buy **2.2637 bitcoins.**

3. By March 1st, the bitcoin price had shot up much higher to **$34.55**. With VA, you would have **sold $39.56** worth of bitcoins (or **1.1449 bitcoins**) to lower your investment value to $300.

When bitcoins were sold, the sale amounts are shown as negative numbers in the table and highlighted in grey. Spending is negative because you receive money from selling bitcoins.

With that out of the way, let's now analyze bitcoin's VA results for 2013...

1. **Net money invested**: the 'net money invested', shown in the bottom half of the table, is **-$4,421.08**. This amount is calculated by adding together all the numbers in the fifth column of the table.

Over 2013, you would have received more dollars from selling bitcoins (negative amounts in the column) than you would have spent buying them (positive amounts). Your net spending, therefore, is a negative number. Put another way, you would have *received* a net amount of $4,421.08 during the year.

Most of this amount came from the sale of 4.0797 bitcoins in December for $3,899.60 after the price of bitcoin increased nearly five-fold during November.

2. **Coins owned at the end of the year:** with VA, you would own **1.2554 bitcoins** at the end of the year. This amount is calculated by adding together all the numbers in the last column of the table.

3. **Percentage return:** even though you would have *received* $4,421.08 overall, you would still have ended up owning 1.2554 bitcoins at the end of the year. Since you effectively got those bitcoins 'for free', we can think of the percentage return as an **'unlimited'** number.

Let's now compare the results of VA from the last page with those of DCA and HODL:

1. **Net money invested**: remember with DCA, you would have invested $100 each month regardless of bitcoin's price. Therefore, the net money invested was $1,200 over the twelve months.

   With HODL, you would have invested $1,200 at the start of the year.

2. **Coins owned at the end of the year**: by investing $100 each month with DCA at the various prices shown in the table, you would have accumulated a total of 22.12 bitcoins after twelve months

   With HODL, you would have spent $1,200 in January buying 90.77 bitcoins for $13.22 each.

   The number of coins owned with DCA and HODL at the end of the year is much higher than the 1.2554 bitcoins for VA. This is expected given that you sell coins with VA when prices are high (and never sell coins with DCA or HODL).

When you sell coins with VA, you lock in profits. This protects you in case prices fall in the future. If you make profits with VA, you can reinvest the cash into other assets like stocks or mutual funds. This will help diversify your overall wealth away from cryptos and ensure you are still earning returns on that cash over time.

3. **Percentage return:** we can calculate the yearly return using the simple formula:

   Return = Value of bitcoins owned at the end of the year / Dollar amount invested during the year

   We can then convert this number to a percentage return:

   % Return = (Return – 1) x 100%

- **Percentage return for DCA:** you owned 22.12 bitcoins at the end of the year. At the December 31st price (shown in the bottom part of the table) of $754.01, those bitcoins were worth $16,678.70 in total.

  You spent $1,200 with DCA, so your return was:

  *DCA return = $16,678.70 / $1,200 = **13.90 times**.*

  As a percentage return, this comes to:

  *DCA % return = (13.90 – 1) x 100% = **1290%.***

- **Percentage return for HODL:** at the year-end price of $754.01, the total value of the 90.77 bitcoins bought with HODL equals $68,441.49.

  Spending $1,200 at the start of the year, the return comes to:

  *HODL return = $68,441.49 / $1,200 = **57.03 times**.*

  This gives a percentage return of:

  *HODL % return = (57.03 – 1) x 100% = **5603%.***

It's clear from the results that each of the three strategies (DCA, HODL and VCA) did remarkably well in 2013. Of course, 2013 was an exceptional year for bitcoin!

With DCA and HODL, you would have finished the year owning many more bitcoins (worth much more dollars) than you would have with VA.

With VA, however, you would have locked in good dollar profits by selling bitcoins when prices were high.

You would have kept those profits regardless of what happened to bitcoin in 2014...

VA Performance 2014

Date	$ Bitcoin price	$ Starting monthly value	$ Value needed each month	$ Invested (+) or received (-)	No. bitcoins bought (+) or sold (-)
Jan 1st	771.40	0.00	100	100.00	0.1296
Feb 1st	832.58	107.93	200	92.07	0.1106
Mar 1st	565.61	135.87	300	164.13	0.2902
Apr 1st	478.38	253.73	400	146.27	0.3058
May 1st	457.76	382.76	500	117.24	0.2561
Jun 1st	630.23	688.38	600	-88.38	-0.1402
Jul 1st	640.81	610.07	700	89.93	0.1403
Aug 1st	594.92	649.87	800	150.13	0.2524
Sep 1st	474.88	638.58	900	261.42	0.5505
Oct 1st	383.62	727.04	1,000	272.96	0.7115
Nov 1st	325.75	849.15	1,100	250.85	0.7701
Dec 1st	379.25	1,280.66	1,200	-80.66	-0.2127

Coins owned Dec 31	3.1641
Year-end price (Dec 31)	$320.19
Year-end coin value	$1,013.13
Net money invested	$1,475.95
Average price per coin	$544.60
VA % annual return	**-31.36%**
DCA % annual return	-36.53%
HODL % annual return	-58.49%

2014 Was a shocker for bitcoin, but the results show that using VA would have:

1. **Limited the loss for the year to 31.36%**, beating both DCA and HODL.

2. **Bought 3.1641 bitcoins during the year on the cheap** - more than you would have with $100 per month DCA (2.3788 bitcoins) or $1,200 with HODL (1.5556 bitcoins).

3. **Took some profits** by selling bitcoins on June 1st and December 1st when the prices had gone by a lot over the previous month.

4. **Spent more money on bitcoins ($1,475.95**) over the year than you would have with DCA and HODL (both $1,200) but paid the lowest average price per coin compared to the other two strategies.

What if you used a spending limit?

Point four above would not apply if you had limited your spending to $1,200 for the year. As shown in the next table, you would have reached the $1,200 spending limit by October, so you would have stopped investing for the year.

If we limit the spending to $1,200, you would have had a larger loss, fewer bitcoins and less profit at the end of the year, but you still would have beaten HODL. You would have done about the same as DCA.

Notice if you add up all the numbers in the 'dollars invested or received' column of the next table you get $1,200. In this example, we could also have made the spending limit higher than $1,200 - say $2,000.

The point of a spending limit is to protect you from investing too much in one crypto coin in a single year. This is because it limits the downside in case an investment keeps going down all year. When using VA, decide on a spending limit (if at all) that's right for you.

VA Performance 2014 (limiting total spending to $1,200)

Date	$ Bitcoin price	$ Starting monthly value	$ Value needed each month	$ Invested (+) or received (-)	No. bitcoins bought (+) or sold (-)
Jan 1st	771.40	0.00	100	100.00	0.1296
Feb 1st	832.58	107.93	200	92.07	0.1106
Mar 1st	565.61	135.87	300	164.13	0.2902
Apr 1st	478.38	253.73	400	146.27	0.3058
May 1st	457.76	382.76	500	117.24	0.2561
Jun 1st	630.23	688.38	600	-88.38	-0.1402
Jul 1st	640.81	610.07	700	89.93	0.1403
Aug 1st	594.92	649.87	800	150.13	0.2524
Sep 1st	474.88	638.58	900	261.42	0.5505
Oct 1st	383.62	727.04	1,000	167.20	0.4358

Coins owned Dec 31	2.3311
Year-end price (Dec 31)	$320.19
Year-end coin value	$746.38
Net money invested	$1,200
Average price per coin	$583.02
VA % annual return	**-37.80%**
DCA % annual return	-36.53%
HODL % annual return	-58.49%

On the next page, we'll revert to having no spending limit to start testing VA for the remaining years...

VA Performance 2015

Date	$ Bitcoin price	$ Starting monthly value	$ Value needed each month	$ Invested (+) or received (-)	No. bitcoins bought (+) or sold (-)
Jan 1st	314.25	0.00	100	100.00	0.3182
Feb 1st	226.97	72.23	200	127.77	0.5630
Mar 1st	260.20	229.28	300	70.72	0.2718
Apr 1st	247.27	285.09	400	114.91	0.4647
May 1st	232.08	375.43	500	124.57	0.5368
Jun 1st	222.93	480.29	600	119.71	0.5370
Jul 1st	258.62	696.06	700	3.94	0.0152
Aug 1st	281.60	762.20	800	37.80	0.1342
Sep 1st	228.12	648.07	900	251.93	1.1044
Oct 1st	237.55	937.20	1,000	62.80	0.2643
Nov 1st	325.43	1,369.94	1,100	-269.94	-0.8295
Dec 1st	362.49	1,225.27	1,200	-25.27	-0.0697

Coins owned Dec 31	3.3104
Year-end price (Dec 31)	$430.57
Year-end coin value	$1,425.37
Net money invested	$718.95
Average price per coin	$217.18
VA % annual return	**98.26%**
DCA % annual return	65.46%
HODL % annual return	37.02%

In 2015, VA:

1. Made a higher percentage return than DCA and HODL.

2. Sold some bitcoins for profit in November and December when prices were high.

3. Bought more bitcoins in February, April, May, June and September when prices were low.

VA Performance 2016

Date	$ Bitcoin price	$ Starting monthly value	$ Value needed each month	$ Invested (+) or received (-)	No. bitcoins bought (+) or sold (-)
Jan 1st	434.33	0.00	100	100.00	0.2302
Feb 1st	373.06	85.89	200	114.11	0.3059
Mar 1st	435.12	233.27	300	66.73	0.1534
Apr 1st	417.96	288.17	400	111.83	0.2676
May 1st	451.88	432.46	500	67.54	0.1495
Jun 1st	536.92	594.10	600	5.90	0.0110
Jul 1st	676.30	755.76	700	-55.76	-0.0824
Aug 1st	606.27	627.52	800	172.48	0.2845
Sep 1st	572.30	755.18	900	144.82	0.2531
Oct 1st	613.98	965.55	1,000	34.45	0.0561
Nov 1st	729.79	1,188.62	1,100	-88.62	-0.1214
Dec 1st	756.77	1,140.67	1,200	59.33	0.0784

Total coins bought	1.5857
Year-end price (Dec 31)	$963.74
Year-end coin value	$1,528.19
Total money spent	$732.83
Average price per coin	$462.15
VA % annual return	**108.53%**
DCA % annual return	84.27%
All in % annual return	121.89%

In 2016, VA:

1. Beat the return of DCA but lost to HODL.
2. Took some profits in July and November when prices were high.
3. Got some good bargains in August and September when prices were low.

VA Performance 2017

Date	$ Bitcoin price	$ Starting monthly value	$ Value needed each month	$ Invested (+) or received (-)	No. bitcoins bought (+) or sold (-)
Jan 1st	998.33	0.00	100	100.00	0.1002
Feb 1st	989.02	99.07	200	100.93	0.1021
Mar 1st	1,222.50	247.21	300	52.79	0.0432
Apr 1st	1,080.50	265.15	400	134.85	0.1248
May 1st	1,421.60	526.27	500	-26.27	-0.0185
Jun 1st	2,407.88	846.89	600	-246.89	-0.1025
Jul 1st	2,434.55	606.65	700	93.35	0.0383
Aug 1st	2,718.26	781.57	800	18.43	0.0068
Sep 1st	4,892.01	1,439.75	900	-539.75	-0.1103
Oct 1st	4,403.74	810.17	1,000	189.83	0.0431
Nov 1st	6,767.31	1,536.72	1,100	-436.72	-0.0645
Dec 1st	10,975.60	1,784.04	1,200	-584.04	-0.0532

Coins owned Dec 31	0.1093
Year-end price (Dec 31)	$14,156.40
Year-end coin value	$1,547.77
Net money invested	-$1,143.50
Average price per coin	-$10,458.83
VA % annual return	**unlimited**
DCA % annual return	646.04%
HODL % annual return	1,318.01%

Like 2013, 2017 was a great year for bitcoin. With VA you would have:

1. Ended up spending less money than you received from the investment over the year, giving you an 'unlimited' investment return.

   Put another way, you would have received $1,143.50 and 0.1093 BTC 'for free'.

2. Ended up owning fewer bitcoins at the end of the year than with DCA (0.6324 BTC) and HODL (1.2 BTC).

   This could protect you if 2018 turns out to be a bad year for bitcoin.

VA vs. DCA and HODL five year comparison: Bitcoin

The below table shows bitcoin's performance with VA, DCA and HODL over the last five years (from 2013 to 2017). For all three strategies, you would have started at the beginning each year:

- With VA, you would start a new $1,200 yearly VA strategy each year ($100 value increases for twelve months in a row). Whatever coins you owned at the end of each year, you would keep invested until the end of the five years.
- With HODL, you would have invested $1,200 at the start of each year. You would not have sold any coins for the whole five years.
- With DCA, you would invest $100 each month for the whole five-year period. Again, you wouldn't have sold any coins here.

VCA vs. DCA and HODL performance (2013-2017)

Year	% Return VA ($1,200 value over 12 months each year)	% Return HODL (investing $1,200 on 1st Jan each year)	% Return DCA (investing $100 each month)
2013	unlimited	5,603.56%	1,290.03%
2014	-31.36%	-58.49%	-36.53%
2015	98.26%	37.02%	65.46%
2016	108.53%	121.89%	84.27%
2017	unlimited	1,318.01%	646.04%
Total bitcoins owned after 5 years	9.43	99.89	4.03
Total dollars spent on bitcoins over 5 years	-$2,636.86	$6,000.00	$6,000.00
Average price paid per bitcoin over 5 years	-$279.77	$60.07	$1,490.25
Value of bitcoins after 5 years at $14,156.40 Dec 31st 2017 price	$133,424.40	$1,414,015.44	$56,996.21
% return	unlimited	23,467%	850%

In terms of percentage return, the previous table shows good results for VA when compared to DCA and HODL. If you had invested in bitcoin using VA over the five years, you would have:

1. **Received $2,636.86 in cash 'for free' from selling bitcoins at high prices.** Put another way, over the five years you would have spent $8,636.86 less than you would have with HODL and DCA (where you would have spent $6,000 with each strategy over the five years).

2. **Accumulated 9.43 bitcoins over the five years, which would be worth $133,424.40 on December 31st, 2017.**

   This result is better than that of DCA, where you would have accumulated less than half the number of bitcoins (4.03) at a total ending value of $56,996.21 by investing $6,000.

   Compared to HODL, however, you would have only accumulated just under one-tenth the number of bitcoins. With HODL, you would own 99.89 bitcoins at a total ending value of $1,414,015.44. It is worth noting that you would have bought most of those bitcoins (90.77 of them) in January 2013.

3. **A percent return that is 'unlimited'.** If we take the percent return to be the main indicator of success, then VA did the best. The return can be thought of as unlimited because you received 'free bitcoins' over the five years.

When analyzing the above results, the key is that with VA your net spending is negative: you would have spent fewer dollars investing than you would have received from selling your bitcoins. This means that even if the price of bitcoin crashed 100% on Jan 1st, 2018, you would still have made a profit from your investment, as you would have received $2,636.36 in net cash from selling bitcoins over the five years.

In other words, with VA you would have taken less risk than with HODL or DCA. You would have less of your total wealth invested in bitcoin because you would have sold coins for profit when prices were high. This would protect the downside in case the price drops later.

Remember, the profits you made from selling bitcoins could have been used for other investments. You could have used the money to invest in other cryptos, or other assets like mutual funds or gold. Doing any of these things would make your wealth less exposed to the returns of bitcoin, which would reduce the overall risk of your investment portfolio by making it more diversified.

VA past performance: Ripple, Litecoin, Dash, Monero and Ethereum

Over the next few pages, I've included some tables to compare the past performance of VA with DCA and HODL for other cryptocurrencies using the same assumptions as we did for bitcoin earlier in this chapter. No spending limit is applied.

The results show a similar pattern...

To get the results you are about to see, I used past pricing data from coinmarketcap.com and a spreadsheet I built to model the results. Not all the above cryptocurrencies have been around as long as bitcoin has, so the results go back as early as possible for each cryptocurrency.

Ripple 2014 (start Jan 1st)

Start and end date	Coin price	
Jan 01, 2014	0.026944	Starting price
Dec 31, 2014	0.024438	Year-end price

	VA	DCA	HODL
Total coins bought	95,549.01	186,663.35	44,536.82
Total money spent	-334.74	1,200.00	1,200.00
Average price paid per coin	-0.003503	0.006429	0.026944
Year-end coin price	0.0244	0.0244	0.0244
Total year-end coin value	2,335.03	4,561.68	1,088.39
Annual Dollar profit / loss	2,669.77	3,361.68	-111.61
% annual return	unlimited	280.14%	-9.30%

Litecoin 2014 (start Jan 1st)

Start and end date	Coin price	
Jan 01, 2014	24.62	Starting price
Dec 31, 2014	2.72	Year-end price

	VA	DCA	HODL
Total coins bought	335.20	167.01	48.74
Total money spent	2,102.43	1,200.00	1,200.00
Average price paid per coin	6.27	7.19	24.62
Year-end coin price	2.72	2.72	2.72
Year-end coin value	911.73	454.28	132.58
Annual Dollar profit / loss	-1,190.70	-745.72	-1,067.42
% annual return	-56.63%	-62.14%	-88.95%

Ripple 2015 (start Jan 1st)

Start and end date	Coin price	
Jan 01, 2015	0.024390	Starting price
Dec 31, 2015	0.00604	Year-end price

	VA	DCA	HODL
Total coins bought	293,398.53	155,148.58	49,200.49
Total money spent	1,884.22	1,200.00	1,200.00
Average price paid per coin	0.006422	0.007735	0.024390
Year-end coin price	0.0060	0.0060	0.0060
Total year-end coin value	1,772.13	937.10	297.17
Annual Dollar profit / loss	-112.09	-262.90	-902.83
% annual return	-5.95%	-21.91%	-75.24%

Litecoin 2015 (start Jan 1st)

Start and end date	Coin price	
Jan 01, 2015	2.7	Starting price
Dec 31, 2015	3.48	Year-end price

	VA	DCA	HODL
Total coins bought	349.85	511.20	444.44
Total money spent	378.85	1,200.00	1,200.00
Average price paid per coin	1.08	2.35	2.70
Year-end coin price	3.48	3.48	3.48
Year-end coin value	1,217.49	1,778.98	1,546.67
Annual Dollar profit / loss	838.64	578.98	346.67
% annual return	221.36%	48.25%	28.89%

Dash 2015 (start Jan 1st)

Start and end date	Coin price	
Jan 01, 2015	1.94	Starting price
Dec 31, 2015	3.27	Year-end price

	VA	DCA	HODL
Total coins bought	576.92	466.98	618.56
Total money spent	1,303.44	1,200.00	1,200.00
Average price paid per coin	2.26	2.57	1.9400
Year-end coin price	3.27	3.27	3.27
Year-end coin value	1,886.54	1,527.03	2,022.68
Annual Dollar profit / loss	583.10	327.03	822.68
% Annual return	44.73%	27.25%	68.56%

Monero 2015 (start Jan 1st)

Start and end date	Coin price	
Jan 01, 2015	0.46576	Starting price
Dec 31, 2015	0.470402	Year-end price

	VA	DCA	HODL
Total coins bought	3,191.25	2,640.82	2,576.43
Total money spent	1,161.22	1,200.00	1,200.00
Average price paid per coin	0.36	0.45	0.4658
Year-end coin price	0.47	0.47	0.47
Year-end coin value	1,501.17	1,242.25	1,211.96
Annual Dollar profit / loss	339.95	42.25	11.96
% Annual return	29.28%	3.52%	1.00%

Ripple 2016 (start Jan 1st)

Start and end date	Coin price	
Jan 01, 2016	0.005955	Starting price
Dec 31, 2016	0.006449	Year-end price

	VA	DCA	HODL
Total coins bought	179,051.03	177,818.30	201,511.34
Total money spent	1,121.40	1,200.00	1,200.00
Average price paid per coin	0.006263	0.006748	0.005955
Year-end coin price	0.0064	0.0064	0.0064
Total year-end coin value	1,154.70	1,146.75	1,299.55
Annual Dollar profit / loss	33.30	-53.25	99.55
% Annual return	2.97%	-4.44%	8.30%

Litecoin 2016 (start Jan 1st)

Start and end date	Coin price	
Jan 01, 2016	3.51	Starting price
Dec 31, 2016	4.33	Year-end price

	VA	DCA	HODL
Total coins bought	306.91	320.52	341.88
Total money spent	1,123.38	1,200.00	1,200.00
Average price paid per coin	3.66	3.74	3.51
Year-end coin price	4.33	4.33	4.33
Year-end coin value	1,328.90	1,387.84	1,480.34
Annual Dollar profit / loss	205.52	187.84	280.34
% Annual return	18.29%	15.65%	23.36%

Dash 2016 (start Jan 1st)

Start and end date	Coin price	
Jan 01, 2016	3.38	Starting price
Dec 31, 2016	11.21	Year-end price

	VA	DCA	HODL
Total coins bought	137.30	184.17	355.03
Total money spent	788.27	1,200.00	1,200.00
Average price paid per coin	5.74	6.52	3.3800
Year-end coin price	11.21	11.21	11.21
Year-end coin value	1,539.13	2,064.51	3,979.88
Annual Dollar profit / loss	750.86	864.51	2,779.88
% Annual return	95.25%	72.04%	231.66%

Monero 2016 (start Jan 1st)

Start and end date	Coin price	
Jan 01, 2016	0.497867	Starting price
Dec 31, 2016	13.78	Year-end price

	VA	DCA	HODL
Total coins bought	139.86	984.81	2,410.28
Total money spent	-2,949.94	1,200.00	1,200.00
Average price paid per coin	-21.09	1.22	0.4979
Year-end coin price	13.78	13.78	13.78
Year-end coin value	1,927.27	13,570.69	33,213.69
Annual Dollar profit / loss	4,877.22	12,370.69	32,013.69
% Annual return	unlimited	1030.89%	2667.81%

Ethereum 2016 (start Jan 1st)

Start and end date	Coin price	
Jan 01, 2016	0.948024	Starting price
Dec 31, 2016	7.97	Year-end price

	VA	DCA	HODL
Total coins bought	142.01	245.21	1,265.79
Total money spent	626.03	1,200.00	1,200.00
Average price paid per coin	4.41	4.89	0.9480
Year-end coin price	7.97	7.97	7.97
Year-end coin value	1,131.83	1,954.34	10,088.35
Annual Dollar profit / loss	505.81	754.34	8,888.35
% Annual return	80.80%	62.86%	740.70%

Ripple 2017 (start Jan 1st)

Start and end date	Coin price	
Jan 01, 2017	0.006368	Starting price
Dec 31, 2017	2.3	Year-end price

	VA	DCA	HODL
Total coins bought	4,693.02	58,917.35	188,442.21
Total money spent	-2,920.70	1,200.00	1,200.00
Average price paid per coin	-0.622351	0.020368	0.006368
Year-end coin price	2.3000	2.3000	2.3000
Total year-end coin value	10,793.94	135,509.89	433,417.09
Annual Dollar profit / loss	13,714.64	134,309.89	432,217.09
% Annual return	unlimited	11,192.49%	36,018.09%

Litecoin 2017 (start Jan 1st)

Start and end date	Coin price	
Jan 01, 2017	4.51	Starting price
Dec 31, 2017	232.1	Year-end price

	VA	DCA	HODL
Total coins bought	12.12	108.06	266.08
Total money spent	-1,627.59	1,200.00	1,200.00
Average price paid per coin	-134.28	11.10	4.51
Year-end coin price	232.10	232.10	232.10
Year-end coin value	2,813.33	25,081.08	61,756.10
Annual Dollar profit / loss	4,440.92	23,881.08	60,556.10
% Annual return	unlimited	1,990.09%	5,046.34%

Dash 2017 (start Jan 1st)

Start and end date	Coin price	
Jan 01, 2017	11.23	Starting price
Dec 31, 2017	1051.68	Year-end price

	VA	DCA	HODL
Total coins bought	1.50	23.03	106.86
Total money spent	-2,670.58	1,200.00	1,200.00
Average price paid per coin	-1,774.89	52.11	11.2300
Year-end coin price	1,051.68	1,051.68	1,051.68
Year-end coin value	1,582.41	24,220.62	112,378.98
Annual Dollar profit / loss	4,252.98	23,020.62	111,178.98
% Annual return	unlimited	1,918.38%	9,264.92%

Monero 2017 (start Jan 1st)

Start and end date	Coin price	
Jan 01, 2017	13.97	Starting price
Dec 31, 2017	349.03	Year-end price

	VA	DCA	HODL
Total coins bought	6.28	42.31	85.90
Total money spent	-2,226.56	1,200.00	1,200.00
Average price paid per coin	-354.28	28.36	13.9700
Year-end coin price	349.03	349.03	349.03
Year-end coin value	2,193.55	14,768.58	29,981.10
Annual Dollar profit / loss	4,420.11	13,568.58	28,781.10
% Annual return	unlimited	1,130.71%	2,398.43%

Ethereum 2017 (start Jan 1st)

Start and end date	Coin price	
Jan 01, 2017	8.17	Starting price
Dec 31, 2017	756.73	Year-end price

	VA	DCA	HODL
Total coins bought	2.57	33.01	146.88
Total money spent	-1,702.95	1,200.00	1,200.00
Average price paid per coin	-662.08	36.36	8.1700
Year-end coin price	756.73	756.73	756.73
Year-end coin value	1,946.41	24,977.53	111,147.61
Annual Dollar profit / loss	3,649.35	23,777.53	109,947.61
% Annual return	unlimited	1,981.46%	9,162.30%

In most cases, VA had a higher percentage return than DCA and HODL. When it did not, it's usually because the price at the start of the year was very low compared to the other prices during the year.

From a risk management perspective, when prices went down over the year, VA did better than DCA and HODL every time. This shows how VA can help lower the risks of crypto investing.

Because we sometimes sell coins with VA, it is the least aggressive strategy out of the three. Although DCA and HODL would often have resulted in you owning significantly more coins at the end of the year (because you would never sell coins), we can't be sure that cryptos will keep going up so much in the next few years. *If we did know this, then HODL would always be the best strategy. If the value of a coin kept going up forever, then it would make sense to never sell!*

But nobody knows what's going to happen tomorrow, so it's better to be safe than sorry by selling some coins when prices are high and buying more coins when prices are low. This way, we profit from volatility - something we *can* be sure of with cryptos.

A commonsense approach, therefore, would be to use VA for the CP strategy. In the next chapter, we'll test VA with diversification to see if we get better results...

 Chapter Summary

1. *As the results show, Value Averaging (VA) seems to reduce the risks of investing in cryptocurrencies like Bitcoin, Ripple, Litecoin, Monero, Dash and Ethereum.*

2. *With VA, you would have done better in 2014 (when prices went down) than you would have with DCA or HODL. Even though the coins went down over twelve months in some cases, you still would have taken profits in some months with VA when prices went up.*

3. *VA doesn't always beat HODL and DCA when prices keep going up. This is because, with VA, you sell coins when prices are high to manage your risks.*

4. *With VA, you could also end up owning fewer coins at the end of the year than you would have with DCA or HODL. While this may sacrifice some potential upside, you are more protected if (when) a market crash happens.*

CHAPTER 12

TESTING VA AND DIVERSIFICATION TOGETHER

"Diversification is an established tenet of conservative investment"

Benjamin Graham

As the results from the last chapter show us, VA can work well on its own to lower the risks of crypto investing. But as we covered in chapter nine, diversification is another great way to reduce investment risk. Using the results from the last chapter for each cryptocurrency, let's now see what the returns from 2014 to 2017 would look like when we add diversification to the mix.

VA with diversification (2014): BTC, XRP & LTC

The table on the next page shows the returns you would have earned if you had split your $1,200 investment equally ($400 in each coin) between bitcoin, litecoin and ripple in 2014. Bear in mind that with VA, your total money spent is less than $1,200 in this case as you would have sold some coins during the year.

Portfolio 2014 (start Jan 1st): BTC, XRP & LTC			
	VA	**DCA**	**HODL**
Total money spent	1,081.21	1,200.00	1,200.00
Year-end portfolio value	1,419.96	1,925.87	573.02
Total Dollar profit / loss	338.75	725.87	-626.98
% Annual return	31.33%	60.49%	-52.25%

Recall from the last chapter that bitcoin went down by 58.49% in 2014. But it wasn't just a bad year for bitcoin - litecoin went down even more (88.95%). Ripple went down too, but only by 9.30%.

By owning equal amounts of all three coins in the diversified HODL portfolio, you would still have lost 52.25% over 2014. This is better than you would have done if you had only owned litecoin, bitcoin, or a combination of both.

In other words, the smaller loss of ripple lowered the overall loss of the diversified HODL portfolio.

But diversification on its own appears to be much more effective when combined with VA or DCA. Even in a down year, the diversified VA strategy returned 31.33%. This is because ripple did very well with VA in 2014 – you would have made more money from selling ripple than you would have spent buying ripple during the year.

With DCA, the portfolio returned 60.49%. The reason it returned more than VA is because of what the price of ripple did in the last two months of the year:

- In November, ripple almost tripled in price. With VA, this resulted in a large sale at the start of December. With DCA, the price didn't matter as you would still have bought ripple.

- In December, ripple doubled in price. But since you would have sold ripple with VA at the start of the month, you would have lost out on some of December's gains. With DCA, however, you would have bought ripple at the start of December.

Even though the DCA portfolio returned more than the VA portfolio, a conservative investor would still have sold some ripple (rather than bought more) at the start of December after it tripled in price.

VA with diversification (2015): BTC, XRP, LTC, XMR & DASH

There's enough past pricing information for 2015 to add Monero and Dash to the portfolios. You would still have invested the same $1,200 in each portfolio overall, but split the different portfolios into five equal parts of $240 in each coin (value for VA and total investment amount for DCA and HODL):

Portfolio 2015 (start Jan 1st): BTC, XRP, LTC, XMR & DASH			
	VA	DCA	HODL
Total money spent	1,089.34	1,200.00	1,200.00
Year-end portfolio value	1,560.54	1,494.17	1,344.53
Total Dollar profit / loss	471.20	294.17	144.53
% Annual return	43.26%	24.51%	12.04%

As shown above, the VA portfolio earned a higher percentage return than the DCA and HODL portfolios. HODL didn't do so well because ripple's price went down by 75.24% in 2015. With VA, however, ripple only lost 5.95% over the year.

VA also did the best with:

- Monero (29.28% return) compared to DCA (3.52%) and HODL (1%).
- Litecoin (221.36% return) compared to DCA (48.25%) and HODL (28.89%).

With Dash, VA earned 44.73%, which was more than DCA (27.25%) but less than HODL (68.56%).

VA with diversification (2016): BTC, XRP, LTC, XMR, DASH & ETH

For 2016, we can add Ethereum to each of the three portfolios:

Portfolio 2016 (start Jan 1st): BTC, XRP, LTC, XMR, DASH & ETH			
	VA	DCA	HODL
Total money spent	240.33	1,200.00	1,200.00
Year-end portfolio value	1,435.00	3,722.57	8,787.42
Total Dollar profit / loss	1,194.68	2,522.57	7,587.42
% Annual return	497.10%	210.21%	632.28%

In terms of percentage return, the VA portfolio beat the DCA portfolio but lost to HODL. With VA, you only would have spent $240.33 buying coins during the year after receiving the cash from selling coins. Again, you could have used the extra money to invest in other assets like stocks, mutual funds or gold to lower the risk of your overall investment portfolio.

VA with diversification (2017): BTC, XRP, LTC, XMR, DASH & ETH

In 2017 everything went up by a lot. Selling coins with the VA portfolio meant more money was received than invested over the year, resulting in an 'unlimited' percent return.

Portfolio 2017 (start Jan 1st): BTC, XRP, LTC, XMR, DASH & ETH			
	VA	DCA	HODL
Total money spent	-2,048.65	1,200.00	1,200.00
Year-end portfolio value	3,479.57	38,918.37	127,616.16
Total Dollar profit / loss	5,528.21	37,718.37	126,416.16
% Annual return	unlimited	3,143.20%	10,534.68%

Of course, you could have turned $1,200 into $127,616.16 using HODL, but 2017 was is an exceptional year for cryptos. Betting that these types of returns will continue would be a gamble.

VA is just one way to invest in cryptos. However, you may be in a position to use HODL if you can afford the risk or have strong conviction that cryptos will continue to boom. In part three of this book, we will look at a few more aggressive crypto strategies that require more work to master but could potentially lead to higher returns.

Final thoughts on VA and diversification

VA doesn't always beat HODL, but it beats it often enough. It also protects the downside and forces you to take some profits when prices are too high for comfort. When we combine VA with diversification, the risks seem to go down even more. Of course, it would be better if we had more years to test these results. But since cryptos are still a new asset class, there unfortunately isn't too much data to work with.

Over the last few chapters, we covered the basic investment strategy of the Crypto Portfolio. The point of the CP is to earn steady gains over time while keeping the risks of crypto investing down as much as possible. This philosophy can apply to all investments, not just cryptos. Provided you don't invest too much money into it, the CP strategy could be a valuable addition to your overall investment portfolio.

Over the next few chapters, we'll look at a few important practical aspects that are more specific to crypto investing...

Chapter Summary

1. *The results of this chapter show that combining diversification with VA could help lower the risks of crypto investing by more than VA alone.*

2. *Interestingly, the diversified VA and diversified DCA portfolios never had a negative year between 2014 to 2017, even though 2014 was a catastrophic year in the crypto market.*

CHAPTER 13

CRYPTO EXCHANGES

"The demand is extremely strong. We opened registration [to Binance] for an hour yesterday and 240,000 users registered."

Zhao Changpeng

Exchanges are your places of business when investing in cryptos, so it's important you choose the right ones for you. There are many to choose from, so in this chapter, we'll try to narrow your choices down.

What is a cryptocurrency exchange?

A cryptocurrency exchange is an online platform which you can use to *exchange* (buy and sell) cryptos with other investors. Some exchanges let you trade *fiat currency* (dollars, euros, pounds, yen etc.) for cryptos. Other exchanges are *crypto only*, meaning you first have to send cryptos (like bitcoin or ether) to them before you can invest in other coins.

Coin prices on exchanges are driven by supply and demand. If there are more investors who want to buy a coin on an exchange than there are who want to sell it, the price of the coin goes up. If there are more sellers than buyers, the price goes down.

If you are using cryptos to buy something (like a loaf of bread for example), you don't use crypto exchanges. Exchanges are purely for trading and investing.

Crypto exchange order matching

Exchanges match buy and sell orders for their customers. If Jessica places a **buy order** for 5 bitcoins, the exchange tries to **fill** her order by matching it with someone who places a **sell order** for 5 bitcoins.

If nobody on the exchange is selling 5 bitcoins, the exchange will then try to **partially fill** Jessica's order by matching it with orders from different sellers. For example, Jake might want to sell 3 bitcoins and Sipho might want to sell 2 bitcoins.

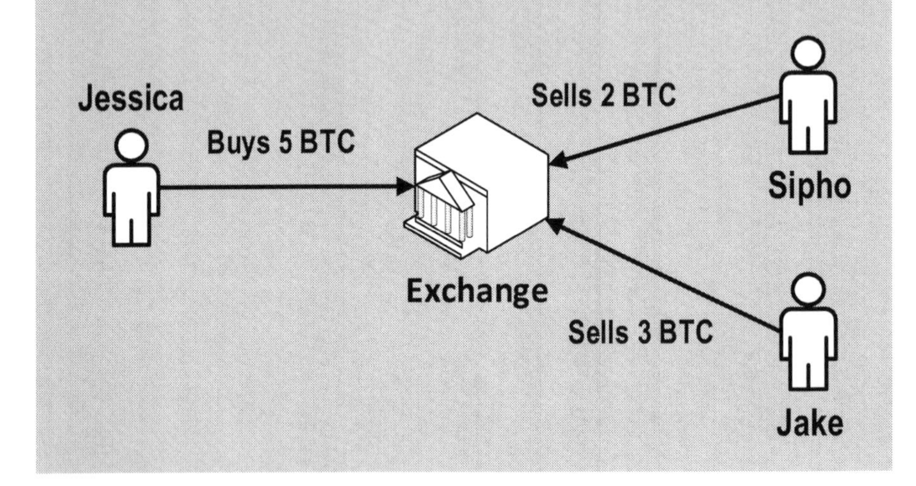

The exchange takes a small fee from both the buyer and the seller in each transaction. These fees vary depending on the exchange but usually range from 0.1% to 1.5% per trade.

Keep an eye on fees when you invest. Over time, high fees can chip away at your investment returns. Exchanges usually charge fees in cryptos, which could be worth a lot one day!

Exchanges do two good things for investors:

1. **Provide liquidity**: since there are lots of people using exchanges, it's easy for investors to find other people to do business with.

2. **Provide coin prices**: as mentioned earlier, supply and demand drive crypto prices on exchanges. Each time a coin is traded on an exchange, its price is updated. The constant stream of trades on exchanges means coin prices change in real time.

That's the basics of how crypto exchanges work. Let's now look at how to choose them...

How to choose exchanges

Here are some questions you can ask yourself before choosing an exchange:

1. Can you use the exchange in your home country?

2. Does the exchange accept deposits in your local currency?

3. Is the exchange secure?

4. Does the exchange have the coins you want to invest in?

5. Does the exchange have reasonable fees and exchange rates?

6. Is the exchange easy to use?

7. Does the exchange have good reviews?

Let's now dive deeper into each of the above points...

1. Exchange country

Cryptos are global, but not all exchanges allow people from every country to use them. Coinbase, for example, is only open to investors in the US, Canada, the UK, Europe, Australia and Singapore[53].

Always make sure the exchange you want to use works in the country where you live.

2. Exchanges and fiat

Some exchanges like Kraken, Bitfinex and Coinbase let you deposit fiat currency (like dollars or euros), which you can then use to invest in cryptos.

Other exchanges, like Bittrex, Binance and Poloniex, only accept cryptocurrency deposits like bitcoin or ether. These *crypto only exchanges* usually have more coins to choose from than crypto exchanges that also accept fiat.

At this point in my life, I use Bittrex, Binance and Kraken. I send fiat (euros) to Kraken and do most of my investing there. I also invest in other cryptocurrencies like Lisk, IOTA, Cardano, EOS, Simple Token, Tronix, Neo and other coins that aren't available on Kraken.

To get funds to Binance or Bittrex:

1. *I buy ether on Kraken with fiat (euros).*

2. *I then send that ether from Kraken to Bittrex or Binance to buy the other coins.*

This is not a recommendation for you to use the same exchanges as me, or to invest in the same coins. It's just what I'm doing.

3. Exchange security

You may have heard about the *Mt.Gox* exchange hack in February 2014, when an unknown hacker stole around 850,000 bitcoins from Mt. Gox's customers. At the time, those bitcoins were worth about $450 million[54]. With many of their customers' accounts emptied, Mt. Gox shut down.

Fortunately, crypto exchanges have significantly improved their security since then. But still, when you store cryptos on exchanges they are not stored in a decentralized way because the exchange holds your money. This means there could potentially be a single point of weakness for a hacker to attack.

Here are some things that make exchanges more secure:

- **Two-factor identification**: after entering your password (one-factor), you enter a number code. With Bittrex, Binance and Kraken, for example, you get the code from an app on your phone such as Google Authenticator. The code is always changing, which means you need your phone with you each time you log in.

- **Cold wallet storage:** sometimes exchanges store coins they don't need for liquidity offline. This means a hacker can't steal those coins by hacking into the exchange's online database. Kraken and Bitstamp do this, for example.

- **Email verification**: if you log on to your exchange account, you get an email to confirm the login. This way, you would know if someone else is trying to access your account.

- **Know Your Customer (KYC):** if an exchange asks you to upload a copy of your passport or driver's license, and asks you security questions when you sign up, that's good. They do this to make sure you're not a dodgy money launderer.

- **Coin insurance**: some exchanges, like Coinbase and Bitstamp, insure most of your coins against theft.

You can better protect yourself on an exchange if you:

1. Have a long password, with lots of numbers, letters and special characters. For every digit your password increases, it becomes exponentially harder to break.

2. Don't use that password for anything else.

3. Use two-factor identification.

4. Only keep crypto coins and fiat currencies on exchanges when you need to. Otherwise, keep them in **cold wallet storage**. We'll cover that in the next chapter.

5. Get verified to the highest **tier** on the exchange. Some exchanges like Kraken and Binance have user verification tiers. If you need to jump through more hoops to get to higher verification tiers, then get jumping!

   Higher verification tiers usually mean you can withdraw more funds (crypto or otherwise) from the exchange in one go. This could be useful if the exchange is having unforeseen security issues and you need to get money out of it quickly.

Be on the lookout for phishing scams in crypto. An example of this could be a malicious website posing as a crypto exchange to steal your login details. Always make sure you enter the crypto exchange website address correctly in your browser before logging into your exchange account.

4. Coins offered on an exchange

Some exchanges offer much more coins than others. For example:

- Bittrex, Binance and Poloniex offer more coins than Kraken.

- But Kraken offers more coins than Coinbase, which only offers Bitcoin, Litecoin, Bitcoin Cash, and Ether.

In chapter eight, you learnt how to choose ten different coins for your CP. Make sure you can buy them on your exchanges. You'll probably need more than one exchange to buy them all. This is a good thing as it will:

1. Get you comfortable using different exchanges.

2. Make sure you don't have too many coins on one exchange at any point in time.

5. Exchange fees and exchange rates

As mentioned at the start of this chapter, exchanges charge fees each time you trade. Other fees could be:

- **Spreads**: this an indirect fee. It's the difference between the price at which you can buy and sell the same coin.

  This is like when you go to a foreign exchange kiosk at the airport. Let's say Mark is a British person who owns pounds and wants to buy dollars from an exchange kiosk in Los Angeles.

  If a dollar costs 0.80 British pence normally, the kiosk charges Mark 0.83 pence for each dollar he buys. He pays more than the *spot rate* of 0.80 pounds per dollar. But if Sally wants to sell dollars for pounds, she only receives 0.77 pence per dollar from the kiosk. She receives less than the spot price. The kiosk is taking a cut of Mark and Sally's transactions - or a *spread*.

  Spreads are, unfortunately, a fact of life with exchanges. More liquid coins usually have lower spreads.

- **Deposit and withdrawal fees**: in some cases, exchanges charge small fees when you deposit or withdraw money. For example, if I move bitcoin from Kraken to Bittrex, Kraken charges me a 0.001 bitcoin fee. If I move ether instead, Kraken charges me 0.005 ether. Based on current exchange rates, moving ether is the cheaper option right now.

- **Bank fees**: if you transfer fiat to an exchange that doesn't accept your local currency, your bank may charge you a fee to send the money internationally. Be aware of this as these fees can add up if you send fiat each month to your crypto exchange.

  If you're worried about this, join a bank that doesn't charge you for international payments!

Fees add up over time and can cut into your investment returns. Make sure your exchange won't overcharge you by reviewing their fee policy before you sign up.

The more you trade, the more fees you'll pay. This is one of many reasons why it's hard to make profits from day-trading. With the CP strategy, you only trade on one day each month. That said, trading fees are usually low for cryptos compared to stocks, for example.

6. Ease of use

If you're new to crypto investing (or investing in general), then most exchanges will look alien to you at first. But like all things, practice makes perfect. Spend a bit of time using different exchanges and everything will become straightforward soon enough.

Some exchanges are easier to use than others. I find Bittrex, Binance, Kraken and Coinbase easy to use - but that's just me.

7. Online reviews

Reviews tell you what other people think about the different exchanges. Most exchanges have *haters* who rant about them, so even the best exchanges have bad reviews. Good places to look for reviews are:

- Reddit forums
- Cryptocompare.com forums

Everyone has an exchange they prefer, so try to find an exchange that suits your circumstances.

At the end of the day, you may need to try a few different exchanges before you decide which ones work best for you. Depending on where you live, here's a list of some reputable crypto exchanges you may wish to consider:

- Coinbase
- Cryptopia
- Kraken
- Binance
- Bittrex
- Bitfinex
- Poloniex

How to use Crypto Exchanges

Each exchange is different, but most of them have a similar setup process where you follow these steps:

1. **Sign up** and go through the various tiers of verification. This usually takes a few business days.

2. **Deposit fiat or cryptos.** This can be instant or a few business days depending on the currency, exchange and method of deposit.

   If you want to send fiat to an exchange but it doesn't accept your local currency, then you may need to do an **international bank transfer** from your online bank account to the exchange.

   For example, I live in the UK and use Kraken. Since Kraken doesn't accept GBP, I send EUR to Kraken's bank in Germany via a **SEPA (Single Euro Payments Area) transfer.** It usually takes one or two business days for the EUR to get to my Kraken account.

3. **Buy or sell cryptos.** Hopefully, this is instant. Bear in mind sometimes orders can take time to fill - especially if the coin you are investing in isn't very liquid.

   When making a trade, you can do a **limit order** or a **market order.** Stick to market orders if you want your trades to go through faster.

   Otherwise, you can use a limit order to set the worst price you would accept for the trade. For example, you could put a limit order to buy BTC for USD 7,000:

- If the BTC price is USD 7,000.50, it will be too expensive, so the buy order won't go through.

- But if the BTC price drops to USD 7,000 or lower, it will be cheap enough, so the buy order will go through.

The limit order will stay in *pending* until it gets executed, or until you cancel it.

Exchanges have interfaces when you log in that show what cryptos and fiat you own at any point in time. They also have **order history** screens to show all the trades you've made.

4. **Transfer crypto coins between exchanges**: if I send coins from Kraken to Binance, Bittrex, or any other exchange, the transfer process is quick (usually less than half an hour) and straightforward. On each exchange, there is a **deposit** and **withdrawal** section.

   To get coins out of Kraken, for example, I click the 'withdraw tab' and go to the currency I want to transfer. Say I want to transfer ether from Kraken to Binance so I can buy Neo:

   - In my Binance account, I have an ether deposit address. I would copy and paste this address into the ether withdrawal section of Kraken.

   - Next, I would send the ether to Binance by withdrawing it from Kraken to my Binance ether deposit address.

When you send coins from one exchange to another, you are doing so via the decentralized blockchain, rather than through the centralized exchanges. This means that you could lose your coins if you get the deposit address wrong. It is, therefore, a good idea to test the process of sending coins from one exchange to another with small amounts before you do any serious transfers.

Final thoughts on exchanges

Before using an exchange, find and watch a **YouTube tutorial** for how that exchange works. This will give you a feel for the user interface of the exchange and explain what you need to do to get set up. Always start with small trades to get used to the exchange before upping the stakes.

You now have enough information to choose your crypto exchanges. Next, we'll explore some of the ways in which you can store your coins...

Chapter Summary

1. *A cryptocurrency exchange is an online platform where you can exchange (buy and sell) cryptos with other investors.*

2. *Some exchanges let you buy cryptos with fiat currency (dollars, pounds, euros etc.). Others are 'crypto only exchanges'. Crypto only exchanges usually have more coins to choose from that 'crypto-fiat exchanges'. You'll need at least one of each type of exchange for your CP.*

3. *When choosing exchanges, make sure they:*

    - *Are secure.*
    - *Are easy to use.*
    - *Have the coins you want in your CP.*
    - *Can be used in your home country.*
    - *Have reasonable fees and exchange rates.*
    - *Have good reviews on reddit.com or cryptocompare.com.*

4. *Crypto exchanges might seem intimidating at first but most of them work in similar ways. If you can use one exchange, learning how to use another is a breeze.*

5. *Sign up to a few different exchanges and see which ones you like. Before you invest any money with them, find and watch YouTube videos that give tutorials on how to use each exchange. You'll be an exchange pro in no time!*

CHAPTER 14

KEEPING YOUR CRYPTOS SAFE

"Safety is a cheap and effective insurance policy"

Unknown

You can have the world's best investment strategy, but if someone steals all your cryptos, you'll lose 100% of your investment. Crypto exchanges have vastly improved their security since the Mt. Gox hack in 2014 and they will continue to do so in the future. But they are still *centralized*, which makes them potentially easier targets for hackers and thieves than decentralized blockchains.

If keeping your coins on exchanges makes you nervous, you can store them in different **wallets**.

What is a crypto wallet?

Unlike the wallet in your pocket, crypto wallets don't store any currency. In fact, the coins aren't physically stored anywhere at all. This is because cryptos are lines of code on a blockchain (or a tangle) stating who owns what.

A crypto wallet is a software program that stores your **public** and **private keys**. Together, these keys let you access your funds and transact on the blockchain.

Public and private keys work together. You can't have one without the other. The next page gives a simple definition of each:

- **Public key**: a long string of numbers and letters that proves you are the owner of your wallet address. It allows you to *receive* cryptocurrency. It doesn't matter if someone else sees your public key.

- **Private key**: an even longer string of letters and numbers that only you can see. It allows you to access your wallet and *send* cryptocurrency to other people. If you lose or forget your private key, you can't access your wallet.

It would take someone 204 Trevigintiilion (or 10 to the power of 72) years to guess your private key with today's computer power. So long as nobody sees your private key, you'll be just fine![55]

Hot vs. cold wallets

Hot wallets store your public and private keys online. They are generally less secure than **cold wallets**, which store them offline. Here are some examples of each:

1. **Hot wallets**: crypto exchanges and software wallets.

   Crypto exchanges mostly store your public and private keys on their computer servers. You can usually unlock your keys with a password and two-factor identification. This allows you to access your account and trade cryptos on the exchange.

   You can download **software wallets** to a computer or mobile phone that is connected to the internet. Some of these, you can only access from the device on which you installed the wallet. Unlike exchanges, these software wallets let you store your own private keys.

   Some software wallets like *blockchain.info* are accessible from any online device. These are more like exchanges because the wallet manufacturer stores your private key. You can access these wallets with a password and extra security measures depending on the wallet.

2. **Cold wallets**: hardware wallets and paper wallets.

   Hardware wallets are portable USB sticks that store your private keys. They are not connected to the internet. You carry them around and connect them to an online computer when you want to transact. They often come with backups, in case you lose your private key.

   A **paper wallet** is another very secure way to store your private key. Depending on the cryptocurrency, the process looks like this:

    1. Go to a secure online piece of software like myetherwallet.com (for Ethereum) or bitaddress.org (for Bitcoin).

    2. Follow the instructions to generate a secure public and private key.

    3. Print the public and private key on a piece of paper. Hide it in a safe place.

The piece of paper you print is the key to unlocking your paper wallet. Never lose it. It's a good idea to have a few printouts stashed in different secure hiding places. Keep them in plastic sleeves so they don't get damaged.

Which type of wallet should you use?

Each type of storage method has advantages and disadvantages. You can choose one that suits your circumstances.

- **Exchanges** are convenient and allow you to store multiple cryptocurrencies depending on the exchange, but they could be a less safe way to store your private keys.

  However, if there's a catastrophic market crash, having coins on an exchange means you can sell them faster - you don't have to first transfer them to an exchange before selling them. Mind you, this type of *panic selling* usually ends badly! Therefore, keeping your coins off the exchange and away from temptation could be the best thing to do.

If you're a more active crypto investor (see part three of this book), then keeping coins on an exchange will help you quickly trade in and out of positions.

- **Software wallets** installed on your computer or phone could be more secure than exchanges but can only be accessed from one device.

- **Online software wallets** can be accessed from anywhere, but you don't control your private keys.

- **Hardware wallets** are secure, easy to use, come with backups and can often store multiple different coins. But they usually cost about $100. Two decent hardware wallets are the *Ledger Nano S* and the *Trezor hardware wallet*.

- **Paper wallets** are secure but not as convenient to use. You usually need a different paper wallet for each cryptocurrency. However, you can in some cases store dApp tokens on the paper wallets of the main dApp platform.

  For example, you can store Ethereum **ERC-20** tokens on myetherwallet.com. ERC-20 tokens are crypto coins used for dApps built on the Ethereum blockchain that comply with a specific set of rules. It's not mandatory for Ethereum dApps to be ERC-20 compliant, so always research online to find the ERC-20 status of an Ethereum dApp coin when looking for possible wallet storage methods.

The more your investments grow, the more steps you need to take to protect your wealth. It is recommended that you use cold wallets as your main source of storage as these are typically more secure than hot wallets. Only keep a small amount of your crypto wealth on exchanges for when you need to trade, and make sure those exchanges are secure! Remember that with the Crypto Portfolio you only trade once a month, so you may want to keep your cryptos in cold wallets when you aren't trading them.

Some exchanges charge you small fees to send coins to other wallets (or other exchanges). Make sure these fees aren't too high. If you're happy with the fees, think of them as small insurance premiums to keep your cryptos safe!

Just like exchanges, there are many different wallet storage methods to choose from. What's more, you often need different wallets for different coins. There's a lot to learn here, but fortunately, you don't need to learn it all straight away. When you start out with your CP, you can store small amounts of cryptos on exchanges (provided they have good security measures) in the short term while you become more familiar with the different wallet options.

Researching online will help you decide which storage methods to use. Visit www.cryptocompare.com/wallets for different wallet reviews. It's also worth finding some YouTube videos that explain how to setup and use each type of wallet. I've included some useful resources at the back of this book if you would like to know more.

It's important to keep your cryptos in the right place. Not just for the reasons I described in this chapter, but also for potentially claiming new coins from forks. More on that in the next chapter!

Chapter Summary

1. *A crypto wallet is a program that stores your public and private keys. Together, these keys let you access your coins and transact on the blockchain.*

2. *Hot wallets store your public and private keys online. This means they are open to potential hacks. Exchanges and software wallets can fall into this category.*

3. *With cold wallets, you store your private keys offline, so they can't be hacked. However, cold wallets can be less convenient to use than hot wallets. You can consider this tradeoff when deciding between hot and cold storage.*

4. *Two types of cold wallets are hardware and paper wallets. Hardware wallets may cost a bit of money, but they're easy to use, highly secure, often store multiple coins and can be backed up in case you lose your private keys.*

5. *Paper wallets are also very secure storage methods, but it's game over if you lose your private key.*

6. *Wallets are intimidating at first as there are lots to choose from. It may take a while to get up to speed in this area, but fortunately, you can temporarily store coins on exchanges in the meantime. Just make sure your exchanges are secure, and that you take security precautions to protect your account.*

CHAPTER 15

WHAT TO DO ABOUT FORKS

"There's no such thing as a free lunch."

Milton Friedman

Recall from chapter five that **hard forks** sometimes create new coins. This can happen when a blockchain splits into two separate chains. If you owned bitcoin at the time Bitcoin Cash was forked, you would have received one bitcoin cash for every bitcoin you owned. The same would have happened if you owned ether when Ethereum Classic was created.

How to claim new fork coins

Not all hard forks create new coins. If they do, it's a bonus! To claim new coins, your original coins must be stored in the right place at the right time.

Storing coins during the fork

In the last chapter, you learnt a few different ways to store your cryptos. This is important when it comes to forks and claiming new coins. Here's what you need to know about forks and each storage method:

- **Exchanges** decide if they will support the fork or not. If they do, you get the new coins very easily by storing the originals on the exchange during the fork. If you plan to keep your coins on an exchange, do some online research ahead of time to see if it will support the fork.

Exchanges sometimes stop you from depositing, withdrawing or even trading the original coin during the fork. This is temporary and is often to protect your coins during the fork.

- **Software and hardware wallets** each have their own processes when it comes to forks. If you control your private key, you decide if you want to claim the new coins (although the process can be complicated at times). If a software wallet provider controls your private key, they decide whether they will support the fork.

  Remember from the last chapter that you control your private key with all hardware wallets, but not all software wallets.

- **Paper wallets**: claiming new coins with paper wallets can be a technical process. This was the case with Bitcoin Cash, as you can see in this article by Luke Stokes on Steemit[56]: www.steemit.com/bitcoin/@lukestokes/safely-claiming-bitcoin-fork-coins-like-bitcoin-cash.

The steps needed to store your original coins and claim new ones will vary depending on the fork, so you need to stay on top of the news. Following websites like stopsaving.com, cointelegraph.com, cryptocompare.com, blockgeeks.com and steemit.com can help keep you up to date.

What to do with your new coins if you get them

The CP strategy is based on rules. You choose ten coins and use VA to buy or sell them each month. But if you get new coins from a fork, you'll own eleven different cryptos. This is a good problem to have!

Here are your options in this case:

1. **Keep the new coins**: investors who held onto bitcoin cash and ethereum classic after each fork made good returns. Bitcoin cash was trading at around $300 on August 2017 and around $1,500 at the time of writing (December 2017). Ethereum classic started at just under $1 in June 2016 and is now about $30.

If you want to hold the coin, do some research to see if it could be a good long-term investment. You can revisit chapter eight for help with this.

2. **Sell the new coins for cash**: if you don't think the new coin is a good long-term investment, you may want to sell it for cash. You can use the money to:

    - **Sell the coins for cash or exchange them for other cryptos as part of your Crypto Portfolio strategy**: This way, you invest less of your 'work money' into your CP over the year.

    - **Sell them for cash and invest in other assets like stocks, bonds or mutual funds**: this is a wise choice - you can potentially earn decent investment returns over time and lower your overall exposure to the crypto market.

New coins are rewarded to investors who take the right steps to get them. If you do get the coins, ask yourself how they can give you the most long-term value. In other words, treat the new coins like you would any other investment.

In the next chapter, we'll go over a topic that is creating enormous confusion and frustration amongst crypto investors...

Chapter Summary

1. *Hard forks sometimes create brand new cryptos like Bitcoin Cash and Ethereum Classic.*

2. *To get the new cryptos, you need to own the original coins at the time of the fork. You also need to store them in the right place at the right time.*

3. *Some exchanges make getting new coins easy by doing all the work for you. Exchanges decide which forks they will support case by case.*

4. *Hard and soft wallets each have their own processes for claiming new coins. Usually, if you have your coins in a hard wallet, you have more chance of claiming them.*

5. *Claiming new coins with paper wallets can sometimes be a technical process.*

6. *Each fork is different when it comes to claiming new coins. Make sure you follow the crypto news (see the resources at the back) to stay updated.*

CHAPTER 16

CRYPTOS AND THE TAX MAN

"There is no such thing as a good tax."

Winston Churchill

Each country has its own way of taxing (or not taxing) crypto returns. If your government doesn't tax them right now, it could decide to later on. Make sure you know the crypto tax situation in your home country. This way, you won't have Uncle Sam knocking on your door when you least expect it.

A bit about Capital Gains Tax

Investors pay **Capital Gains Tax (CGT)** on any profits or *gains* from selling their investments. Before we get to crypto CGT, let's first take a look at the below example to explain how CGT works:

Capital Gains Tax (CGT)

Assume:

1. Katrina buys a painting for $1,000.

2. She sells it for $1,300.

3. She lives in the land of Taxvaria, whose government charge a 10% tax on capital gains.

Katrina's capital gain on the painting is $300 ($1,300 - $1,000). Therefore, she pays $30 (10% of $300) to the Taxvarian government.

If Katrina were to HODL her painting forever, she wouldn't pay any CGT. She only pays tax once the profits are 'realized' after the sale.

Some countries have **capital gains tax allowances.** This means investors can earn some amount in capital gains without being taxed. In the UK, for example, investors can earn up to £11,100 each year in tax-free capital gains. Only the gains that go over this limit are taxed.

How to record capital gains for the tax man

The more capital gains profit you make, the more CGT you pay.

The amount of profit you record depends on two things:

1. How much you **sold** the investment for. For tax reasons, the sale price is set in stone - there's only one way to record it. If you sell a coin for £100, that's what goes in your records.

2. How much you **bought** the investment for. Depending on the country where you live, you may have some flexibility in how you record this. Say you bought five coins at different times throughout the year. Each time, the price was different. If you sell a coin for £100, the profit you record depends on which of those five coins you are selling.

Depending on the laws of your land, here are four potential methods to record capital gains profits for tax reasons.

1. **FIFO (First-in-First-Out)**: you take the profit from your first trade.

2. **LIFO (Last-in-first-out)**: you take the profit from your last trade.

3. **Weighted Average Cost**: you take the profit from an average of all your trades during the year.

4. **Specific Identification**: you choose which trade to take the profit from.

The below example dives into each of these in more detail...

Recording capital gains for tax reasons

Assume:

1. Lorenzo is a crypto investor who lives in Taxiccily.

2. The Taxiccilian Revenue Service taxes all crypto gains at 10%.

3. In Taxiccily, investors can record their profits using the FIFO, LIFO, Weighted Average Cost, or Specific Identification method.

Lorenzo only invests in *ProfitCoin (PC)*. Over the last year, he made the below four trades on PC:

Date	Buy or Sell?	Number of PC Coins	Price per coin	Trade value
Jan 1st	Buy	1	$100	$100
Feb 1st	Buy	2	$50	$100
Mar 1st	Buy	1	$140	$100
Apr1st	Sell	2	$150	$300

Lorenzo needs to submit a tax return but can't decide which tax method to use to record his profits. Let's now go through each method to see which one he should use.

1. FIFO (First-in-first-out)

Lorenzo sold 2 PCs in April at $150 each, giving him $300 in revenue. With the FIFO method, he needs to record a sale of the first 2 coins he bought.

He bought his first coin in January for $100. He then bought 2 more coins in February for $50 each. Since he sold 2 coins overall, he only needs to record 1 coin from February in the sale – the rest of the profit comes from the coin he bought in January. The total value of the first 2 coins he bought is $150, or:

- 1 Coin for $100 (January), plus
- 1 Coin for $50 (February).

Lorenzo's taxable gain is, therefore, **$150** ($300 revenue - $150 paid for coins). Given the 10% tax rate, he owes **$15 in tax** (10% of $150) to the Taxiccilian Revenue Service.

2. LIFO (Last-in-last-out)

With LIFO, Lorenzo records the sale of the last 2 PC coins he bought. Therefore, his total cost for the sale comes to $190, or:

- 1 Coin for $140 (March), plus
- 1 Coin for $50 (February).

He records a **$110** taxable profit (£300 revenue - $190 paid for coins), which means he pays **$11** (10% of $110) in tax.

3. Specific Identification

With this method, Lorenzo can choose or *specifically identify* which coins he sold. If he wants to pay the least amount of tax, he should sell the two most expensive coins to get the lowest taxable profit.

- The most expensive coin is the one he bought in March for $140.
- The second most expensive coin is one of the coins he bought in January for $100.

Adding these up, his total cost for the sale comes to $240. He records a **$60** taxable profit ($300 revenue - $240 paid for coins), so he only pays **$6** (6% of $60) in tax.

4. Weighted Average Cost (WAC) Method

For Lorenzo to use the WAC method, he needs to find the average price he paid per PC coin over the 3 months. Before he sold his 2 PC coins, Lorenzo bought:

- 1 Coin in January for $100.
- 2 Coins in February for $50 each.
- 1 Coin in March for $140.

Overall, he bought 4 coins (1 in January + 2 in February + 1 in March) for $340 ($100 in January + $100 in February + $140 in March). The average price he paid per coin is therefore:

Average price per coin = $340 / 4 = $85

Lorenzo sold two coins for $85 each, which comes to $170. He records a **$130** taxable profit ($300 revenue - $170 paid for coins) and has a **$13** tax bill (10% of $130).

Which profit recording method do you use?

In the above example, the Specific Identification method saves Lorenzo the most money on tax. With this method, he sold the most expensive coins to give him the lowest taxable profit.

The method you use will depend on the tax laws of your home country. It's worth speaking to a tax consultant to research this further.

Netting losses against gains

With **Value Averaging**, you only sell coins at a profit. You buy low and sell high. But sometimes, you may need money for an unforeseen emergency. If that happens, you may need to sell some of your investments at a loss.

In this case, the loss would lower your overall taxable profit for the year, which would lower your tax bill.

Losing money on other investments, such as stocks, would also lower your overall capital gains tax bill for the year.

Crypto taxes in the UK and the US

To explain how cryptos are taxed in most countries would need its own book, so I'll only briefly go over the UK and the US here. If you're not from either of these countries, I apologize and encourage you to look into this further or speak to a local tax consultant. If you are from the UK or the US, research this more anyway, as tax rules can change at any time!

Crypto tax in the United Kingdom

Her Majesty's Revenue and Customs (HMRC) treat bitcoin and other cryptocurrency investments as either:

1. **Foreign currency investments**, where you pay capital gains tax in the same way as you would for stocks and other taxable investments[57], or

2. **Speculative trading transactions,** like gambling, where you don't pay any tax. With gambling, you can also lose a lot of money, which you could offset against profits to pay less tax overall. HMRC doesn't like that.

On the HMRC website[58], it says that taxes on cryptocurrency profits "will be considered on the basis of its [their] own individual facts and circumstances".

In other words, if you think investing in cryptos is gambling, then you can try not pay any tax. As a U.K investor myself, and the author of a book about how to sensibly invest in (rather than gamble on) cryptos, I'm personally going to pay all the tax I might owe.

Remember, UK citizens have an £11,100 capital gains tax allowance. If you are a UK citizen, make sure to use your allowance!

Crypto tax in the United States

The *Inland Revenue Service (IRS)* treats cryptos as property for tax reasons[59]. All US crypto investors must pay capital gains tax on their profits.

By default, US crypto investors must use FIFO *unless* they can prove "adequate identification", in which case they can use LIFO or Specific Identification. Here's what it says in the Treasury regulation 1.1012-1(c)(2) -(4) [60]:

> "An adequate identification is made if it is shown that certificates representing shares of stock from a lot which was purchased or acquired on a certain date or for a certain price were delivered to the taxpayer's transferee... Where the stock is left in the custody of a broker or other agent, an adequate identification is made if— (a) At the time of the sale or transfer, the taxpayer specifies to such broker or other agent having custody of the stock the particular stock to be sold or transferred, and (b) Within a reasonable time thereafter, confirmation of such specification is set forth in a written document from such broker or other agent.... I[I]n the case of a sale or transfer of a book-entry security..., pursuant to a written instruction by the taxpayer, a specification by the taxpayer of the unique lot number which he has assigned to the lot which contains the securities being sold

or transferred shall constitute specification as required by such subparagraph."

This is where things get hazy. If I were American, I would either hire a tax consultant or use FIFO and move on!

Keeping records of your trades and profits

Cryptos are still a grey area when it comes taxes, but it would be wise to prepare for the worst. Besides, having to pay taxes on your profits is a good problem to have - it means your investment strategy is working!

Regardless of whether your government taxes your precious crypto profits or not, you need to keep records of what you're doing. Here's why:

1. Your government can (and probably will) change how it taxes cryptos in the future. Good record keeping prepares you for any scenario and could save you a lot of pain and money (in tax fines) in the future.

2. Good record keeping means you can instantly analyze how your crypto investments are doing. You can see which investments are paying off and which ones aren't.

You can keep records of your monthly CP trades in an excel spreadsheet, or you can read the next chapter for a great alternative...

The VA spreadsheet I mentioned in chapter ten, which you can download at www.stopsaving.com/blog/my-crypto-investing-strategy, uses Weighted Average Cost to calculate profits. This spreadsheet is not meant for taxes, it's only to automate VA calculations each month.

Chapter Summary

1. *Depending on what your local tax man says, you may have to pay Capital Gains Tax (CGT) on your crypto returns.*

2. *With CGT, a percentage of any gains you make over what you invested goes to the tax man. The percentage varies by country.*

3. *Depending on where you live, you may be able to report gains for tax reasons using the FIFO, LIFO, WAC or Specific Identification methods.*

4. *If you lose money on one investment, your total capital gain goes down, so you pay less tax. This applies to all investment used for CGT, not just cryptos.*

5. *Some countries like the UK have CGT allowances. This means some of your gains can be tax-free.*

6. *If your government doesn't tax crypto returns right now, it may decide in the future, so always keep records of what you're doing. This way, you will be prepared for any scenario Uncle Sam throws your way!*

CHAPTER 17

KEEPING TRACK OF YOUR CRYPTO PORTFOLIO

"If you can't measure it, you can't improve it."

Peter Drucker

With so many different exchanges and wallets, crypto investing can be messy. Fortunately, **cryptocompare.com** makes it easy for you to keep track of your crypto investments. You can sign up to and use CryptoCompare for free. Just like with Facebook, Instagram and Linkedin, you choose a username and upload a profile picture.

CryptoCompare has a few things that make it useful for crypto investing. These include crypto chat forums, exchange and wallet reviews, price charts and descriptions of different coins. In this chapter, we'll focus on its portfolio tracking tool.

The CryptoCompare portfolio tracking tool

To keep track of your investments from one place, you can replicate your CP with the **portfolio tool.** Each time you buy or sell coins on any exchange, you add a trade to your portfolio on CryptoCompare. The portfolio tool combines these trades to make a price graph of your CP that changes with the values of your coins.

Crypto prices feed into CryptoCompare from lots of different exchanges[61], so the value of your portfolio changes in real time. Every second of every day, you have a snapshot of how your investments are doing. We'll explore the different features of this later in this chapter.

How to start a portfolio on CryptoCompare.com

After you sign up, go to the portfolio section of the website. Here, you can add a new portfolio to your CryptoCompare account by clicking the **+ portfolio button**. The below screenshot shows what this looks like:

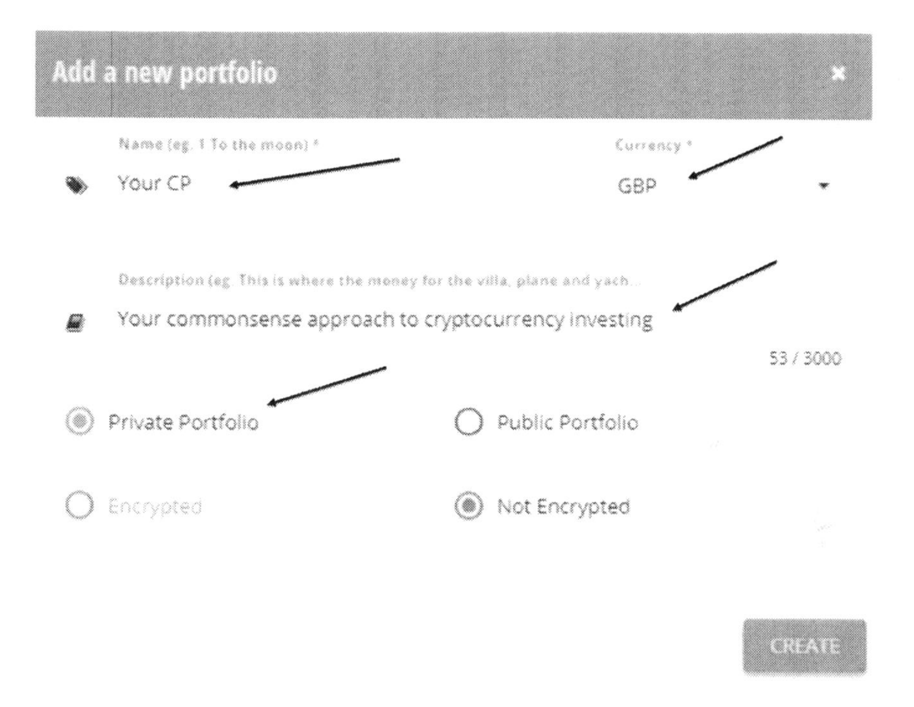

As shown above, choose a name for your CP, give it a description and enter the currency you want your portfolio to be measured in. You can then decide whether you want your portfolio to be public (so anyone can see it) or private (so only you can see it). Note that you can edit any or all of these details later on.

We'll now go over an in-depth example to show how the CryptoCompare portfolio tool works.

Using the CryptoCompare portfolio tool

On January 1st, 2018, Sam sets up a portfolio on CryptoCompare to keep track of his past investments. He calls it *Sam's Crypto Portfolio*.

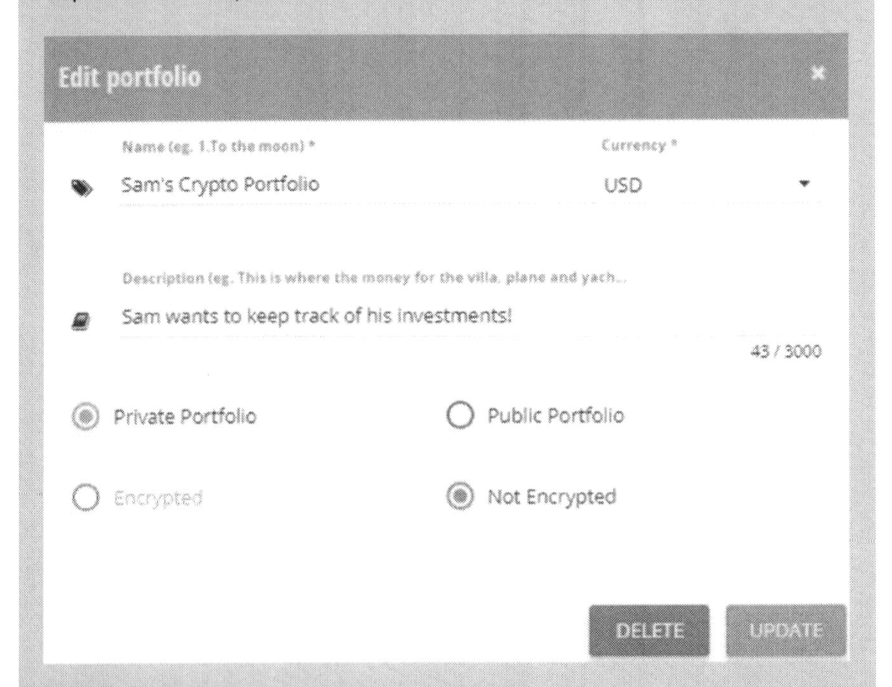

For this example, the prices used approximate real prices in the crypto market at the times of each of Sam's trades. The results you are about to see are exceptional given the strong bull market that took place in 2017. It won't always be like this. Crypto markets have extreme downturns too. As always, past performance is no indication of future returns.

1. Recording purchases

4 Months ago, on September 1st, 2017, Sam bought:

- 1 Litecoin for $80 on the Coinbase exchange.
- 1 Ether for $400 on the Bitfinex exchange.

- 1 Monero for $150 on the Kraken exchange.

Sam clicks the **+ Coin button** to add the 1 LTC he bought on Coinbase in September to his portfolio. He adds the description “Buy 1 Coinbase” to remind him later that this was his first Litecoin purchase for his portfolio, and that he made the trade on Coinbase.

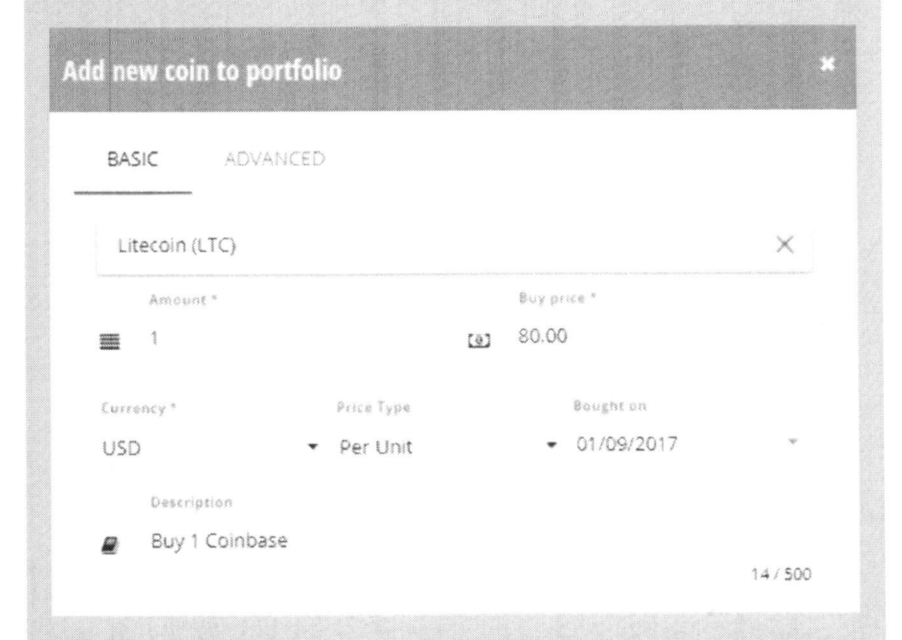

*In the ‘advanced tab’ shown above, Sam can say whether his 1 LTC is stored in a wallet or on an exchange. This information feeds into the **risk analysis section** of his portfolio. We’ll go over this in more detail at the end of this example.*

Next, Sam’s portfolio updates to reflect the trade:

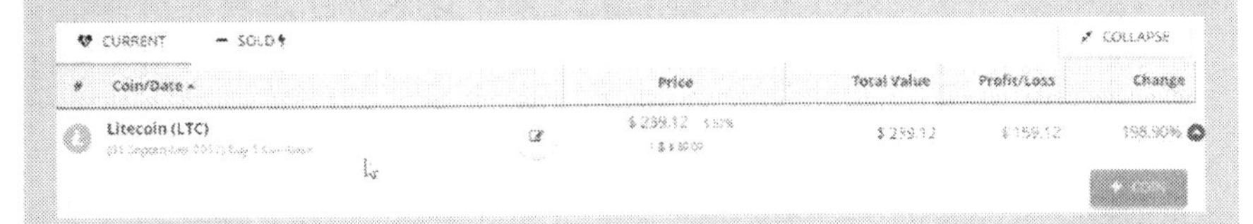

Sam does the same thing for the other two purchases he made in September. He can now see all three trades and how each one has performed since he first invested his money:

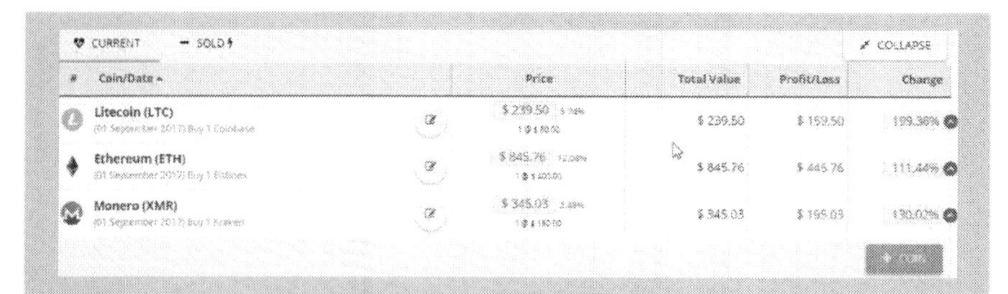

Sam can also see a graph of how his portfolio has done so far:

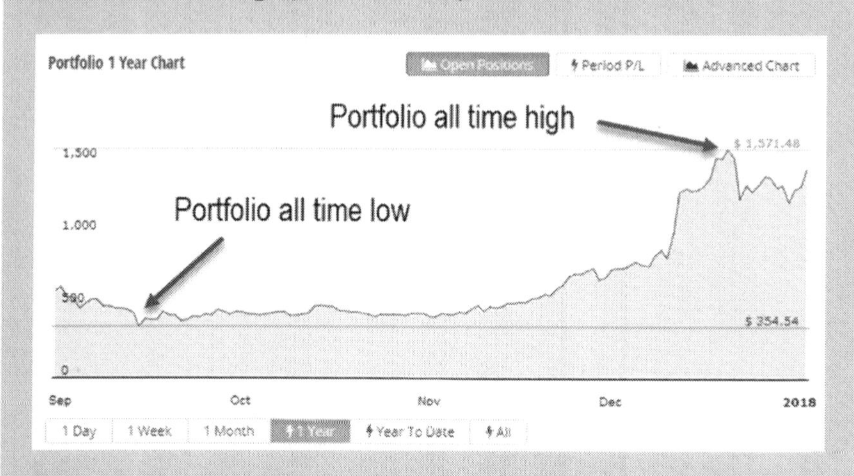

Sam recalls that he also bought coins on October 1st:

- 1 Litecoin for $54 on Coinbase.
- 1 Ether for $300 on Bitfinex.
- 1 Monero for $100 on Kraken.

He adds the above trades to his portfolio. He can now see all his trades over the two months and the profit (or loss) from each trade:

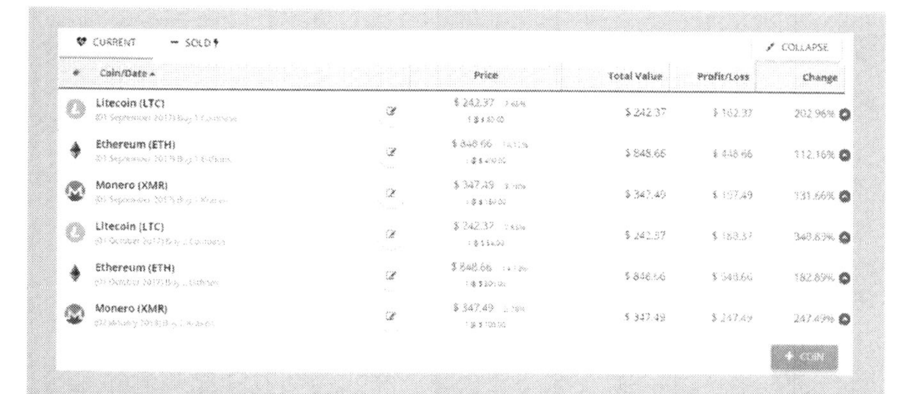

The portfolio graph now also updates to show the change:

2. *Recording sales*

Sam remembers that, on November 1st, he sold 1 ETH for $300. Sam uses FIFO for tax reasons, so he sold the first ether he bought (the one from September, which cost him $400).

To add the sale to his Portfolio, Sam clicks the **edit button** on his September ETH purchase:

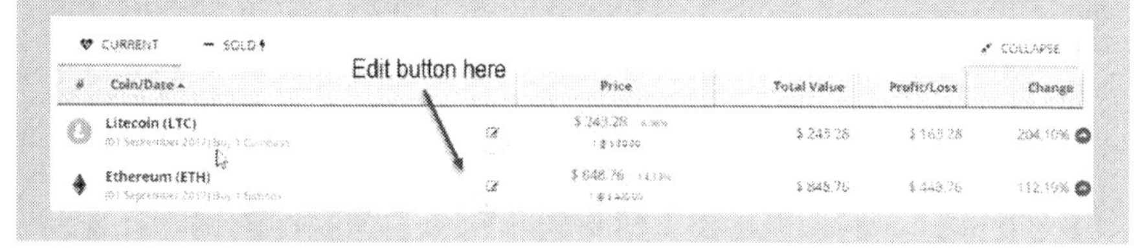

He adds the description “Sale (FIFO)” for his records:

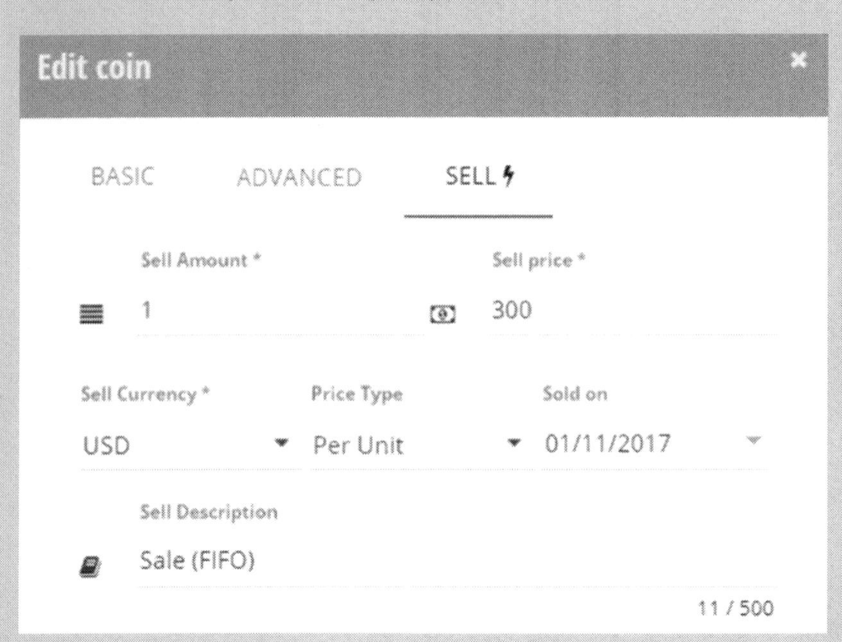

Under FIFO, Sam made a $100 loss on the sale. This is because he sold 1 ETH for $300 in November and bought it for $400 in September.

After he updates the sale, it shows up on the **sold tab** of his portfolio:

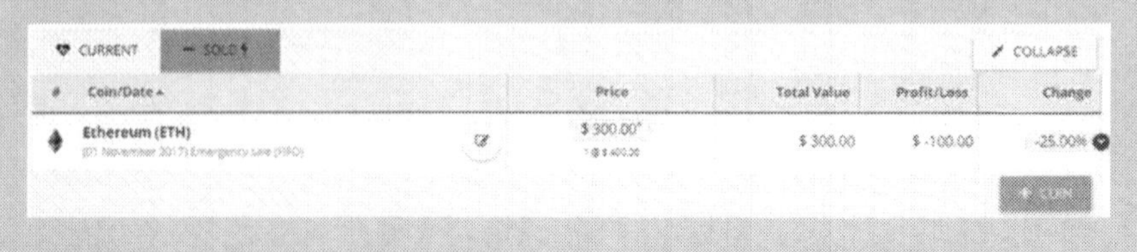

The graph of Sam’s portfolio then updates to reflect the sale:

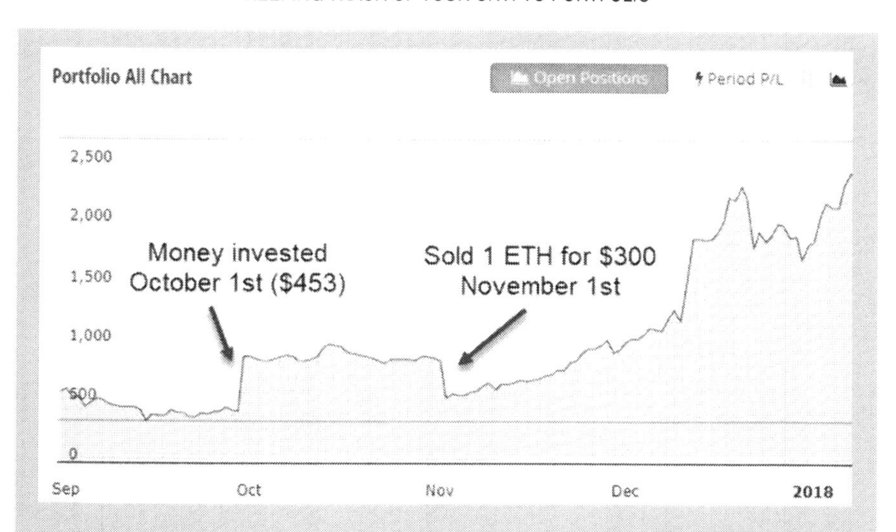

The above graph shows how the total value of Sam's portfolio changes over time. The value goes up and down depending on the performance of Sam's investments. It also goes up when he buys cryptos, and down when he sells them. This explains the vertical lines shown in October and November when Sam made his buy and sell trades.

3. Accounting

After the sale, Sam checks the **accounting section** to see how much money has gone in and out of his portfolio. Here's what he sees:

Income statement

Item	Amount
Total Investment On Sold Positions	$ 400.00
Total Revenue	$ 300.00
Realized P/L	$ -100.00
Capital Gains Tax (%)	12
Amount Exempt From Tax	0
Tax Payable	$ 0

Cashflow statement

Item	Amount
Total Investment	$ 1,084.00
Total Revenue	$ 300.00
Net Cashflow	$ -784.00

- The **income statement** shows the total income and profit on Sam's portfolio. Notice above that the **realized P/L** is -$100 after he sold 1 ETH at a $100 loss.

- The **cashflow statement** shows how much money has gone in and out of his portfolio. Sam invested a total of $1,084 over the two months. After he sold 1 ETH, he made $300 in revenue. His **net cashflow** is, therefore, -$784. This means he has spent $784 after subtracting the $300 revenue from the sale.

When recording gains and losses for taxes, make sure you use the right profit recording method (for example FIFO or LIFO) and the tax rate of your home country.

4. Checking portfolio performance

At any point in time, Sam can see how his portfolio is doing. He now glances above the graph on his portfolio for more information:

Acquisition Cost	Realized P/L	Profit / Loss	Holdings	24H Profit / Loss
$ 684.00	$ -100.00	$ 1,332.22 ▲ 194.77%	$ 2,016.22	$ 132.49 ▲ 7.03%

As shown above, he can see the:

- **Acquisition cost**: how much he has invested overall. When Sam sold the ETH he bought for $400, his total acquisition cost would have gone down by $400.

- **Realized profit and loss**: how much profit or loss he has (or doesn't have) in the bank.

- **Profit and loss**: how much his portfolio is up or down. This excludes the $100 loss from selling 1 ETH. If Sam were instead $100 in realized profit, the profit and loss figure would exclude this too.

- **Holdings**: the value of his coins that he hasn't sold yet. This also excludes the realized profit and loss.

- **24 Hour profit and loss**: how much profit or loss he has made over the last 24 hours.

5. Portfolio risk analysis features

In the **risk analysis** section, Sam can see his portfolio's:

- **Wallet/exchange exposure:** where his coins are stored. Sam can edit each buy trade to say whether he stores those coins on a wallet or an exchange. The wallet/exchange exposure feature gives Sam a percentage split between the two storage methods.

- **Crypto exposure:** the percentage of Sam's portfolio in each coin. This changes with time as each investment earns him a different return. For example, let's say Sam has just two coins in his portfolio, ETH (50%) and LTC (50%). If ether's returns go up more than litecoin's, his portfolio now has more than 50% in ether and less than 50% in litecoin.

- **Liquidity exposure:** the risk of Sam not being able to sell a coin because there aren't enough people to buy it from him. Luckily, Sam owns litecoin, ethereum and monero, which are all very liquid. If he owned lesser known and smaller cap coins, his liquidity risk could go up.

- **Volatility exposure:** the risk of Sam's portfolio moving up or down in price by a large amount in a short space of time. Diversifying into more than three different coins could lower this risk for Sam.

As part of my research for this book, I set up a public portfolio on CryptoCompare in September 2017 to test the CP strategy for six months. You can view the portfolio at www.cryptocompare.com/portfolio-public/?id=87342. This portfolio is not meant to be investment advice, it's just for illustration! I also wrote about the strategy I used for my public CryptoCompare portfolio in this blog post: www.stopsaving.com/blog/my-crypto-investing-strategy.

Final thoughts on CryptoCompare

The CryptoCompare portfolio tool is useful for anyone using the CP strategy, or any other crypto investing strategy for that matter. Aside from having a great tool to track your portfolio, CryptoCompare has descriptions of all the different coins, wallet and exchange reviews, price references and charting software. It also has forums where you can chat with other crypto investors. These can all improve your knowledge and understanding of cryptocurrency investing.

In the next chapter, we'll round up part two of this book with an action plan for your CP strategy!

Chapter Summary

1. *The CryptoCompare portfolio tool can help you keep track of your crypto investments from one place. This is useful if you use different crypto exchanges and wallets.*

2. *Other features of the portfolio tool are:*

    - *Portfolio accounting to check your profit and loss.*
    - *Portfolio risk analysis features to check where your portfolio is at the most at risk.*

3. *Aside from the portfolio tool, CryptoCompare has a few other things which make it useful for crypto investors:*

    - *Descriptions and prices for most of the different coins in the market.*
    - *Wallet and exchange reviews.*
    - *Chat forums for chatting with other investors.*
    - *Charting software for the different coins to analyze price movements.*

CHAPTER 18

BRINGING IT ALL TOGETHER: YOUR CRYPTO PORTFOLIO ACTION PLAN

"It is in doing things and not reading about them that results come about"

Stephen Richards

So far in this book, we've picked up lots of pieces of the crypto puzzle. Now, it's time to put that puzzle together with an action plan for your CP.

Here's a nine-step summary of what you need to do:

1. **Decide how much money (if any) you can afford to invest in your CP over the next year**. This will be the *maximum* amount you'll invest over the next twelve months using the VA strategy (see point four below).

   Remember, with VA, you could end up investing less than your maximum over the year if your crypto investments go up. But if they go down, you could end up investing more than you would like to. This is why you could set a maximum investment limit if you want to. The higher your risk tolerance, the higher your limit should be. You can decide on a limit that fits your **ability** and **willingness** to take risk.

   You can base this decision on:

   - Your current financial situation.

- Your desired investment split between different assets like mutual funds, gold, or buy-to-let property. Remember, always invest less money in riskier assets (like cryptos) and more in safer assets, like diversified mutual funds.

It goes without saying that cryptos are risky investments, so only invest what you can afford to lose!

2. **Choose ten crypto investments for the year.** Base this decision on the *Market cap method*, the *Coingecko method*, or the *Gecko-Market cap method*. Even better, use these methods as a first screening to narrow your choices down. Then, do further research to choose your ten coins.

   Take your time but don't over think it - there's no such thing as the perfect portfolio.

3. **Sign up to a reputable crypto exchange** where you can deposit fiat (dollars, euros, pounds etc.) and buy or sell most if not all your ten coins. If you can't trade some of the coins in your CP with fiat, you'll need to sign up to a second exchange that trades those coins.

   You will then need to follow the below steps each month to buy the coins that aren't on your *fiat - crypto exchange*:

   1. Buy bitcoin or ether from your fiat exchange.

   2. Send that bitcoin or ether to your second *crypto only exchange*.

   3. Once that bitcoin or ether gets to your second exchange, use it to buy the remaining coins in your CP.

   Go through *all* the security tiers for each exchange you use to get verified to the highest tier. The more verified you are, the better. *Note that it can be slower to withdraw money from exchanges if you are not verified to the highest tier!*

4. **Calculate your desired monthly value increases of your CP each month for VA.** As per point one above, chose the maximum value

you want to be invested in your CP at the end of the year. Now, divide that number by 12 to get the monthly value increases.

For example, if you want to own £2,400 worth of cryptos by the end of the year, you would need monthly value increases of £200 (£2,400 divided by 12) for your CP.

Next, divide this number by 10 to get your desired monthly value increase for each coin in your CP. For example, if you want your CP to increase by £200 each month, you get £20 (£200 divided by 10) value increases for each coin in your portfolio. This may not seem like much in each coin, but over time it could make a big difference to your finances. Don't try to get rich quick. Patience is a virtue – especially when it comes to investing.

If you need a spreadsheet to make your monthly VA trades easier to track, read my blog post at the link below, where you can download the spreadsheet for free. The blog also explains how to use the spreadsheet and summarizes how the CP strategy works.

www.stopsaving.com/blog/my-crypto-investing-strategy

5. **Consider wallet options to make sure your cryptos are safe.** There's a tradeoff here between safety (cold wallets) and convenience (exchanges). The larger your CP gets, the more reason to keep your coins in cold wallets.

6. **Watch out for new 'fork coins'**. If there's a fork coming up that's going to dish out new coins, weigh up the amount of effort needed against the potential value of the new coins.

   If you get new coins from the fork, do some more research to decide if you want to hold them or sell them for cash. If you sell them, it's a good idea to use the money to invest in other assets like mutual funds or put it towards your monthly VA Crypto Portfolio payments.

7. **Stay on top of the crypto tax situation in your home country.** Find out if you can use FIFO, LIFO, Weighted Average, Specific Identification or some other method not covered in this book. Ask a tax consultant if you're unsure which method (any any) to use.

If your government doesn't tax crypto returns right now, prepare for the worst by keeping full records of all your trades and capital gains and losses. Always set money aside to pay taxes on your crypto returns if (when) your government starts taxing them.

8. **Sign up to cryptocompare.com to keep track of your CP**. Record every trade. You can also use this resource to find out more about wallets, exchanges and much more.

9. **Get on with your life!** I know it's tempting but try not to look at your portfolio every day. In the long run, you could be better off for it - both financially and emotionally.

What to do twelve months from now

Once twelve months of VA is up, you can then decide if you want to:

1. Extend your CP strategy for another year using the same ten coins. Or,

2. Start a new CP based on what you think are the best ten coins at that time. Since the crypto market is always changing, this may be the better choice. It may also be a good idea to keep most of the coins but only make one or two changes. One year from now you will be a more experienced crypto investor, so you'll be more confident choosing coins.

If you start a new CP, you can keep the old one invested. Just make sure to take profits from it occasionally if you get them - you don't want to end up with too much of your total wealth in the crypto market. If you own other assets besides cryptos (you should), **rebalancing** your overall portfolio each year is an easy way to do this.

As mentioned in chapter seven, rebalancing is when you restore the original split of your investment portfolio by:

1. Selling some of your investments that went up, and

2. Using that money to buy more of the investments that went down.

Final words on the CP strategy

The CP strategy is a simple and effective way to invest in cryptos while spending very little time in front of your trading screen. There are no guarantees when it comes to investing, but by using the CP strategy you could earn good investment returns over time without taking too much risk.

It won't always be smooth sailing but taking a sensible approach to crypto investing (and investing in general) could make a big difference to your financial situation further down the road. Remember, the journey to the moon is long and dangerous. But if you manage the risks and keep learning as much as you can, I'm sure you'll get there in the end!

I wrote this book to explain what cryptos are and how to make investing in them easy and effective for you. I hope I've achieved this with the CP strategy. With that said, I realize some people may want to take a more active approach to crypto investing.

If that's you, you might enjoy what's up next in part three of this book.

If not, it's still worth reading part three to build your crypto investing knowledge further!

PART 3: ADVANCED CRYPTO TRADING AND INVESTING STRATEGIES

CHAPTER 19

THE DARK ARTS OF TECHNICAL ANALYSIS

"Technical analysis works precisely because people look at it. And if people care, I care."

John Bollinger

Technical Analysis (TA) or *chart wizardry* is when you look at past price and volume patterns in charts to try and predict what's going to happen next. This can help you decide whether to buy or sell. TA can be good for short-term traders looking to profit from sharp movements in the market, or longer-term investors looking to buy low and take profits on the way up. There's a lot to learn here, so we'll only cover some of the basics of TA in this chapter.

TA and trend spotting

"The trend is your friend" is a common saying amongst traders and investors, especially those using TA. Trends go up or down depending on how investors feel about an investment over a period of time. When a trend forms, it can become a self-fulfilling prophecy as more investors jump on the trend. Here are two simple examples of this:

1. Bob sees Ripple going up steadily today (the trend is up).

2. He gets FOMO and buys Ripple.

3. Joe, Sally and Fred all do the same, so the price of Ripple goes up more.

4. Dave, Xavier and Molly then buy Ripple too, and the price goes up even more.

Or...

1. Lisa sees Monero dropping (the trend is down).

2. She panics and sells her Monero.

3. Jess, Abu and Diego do the same, so the price of Monero goes down more.

4. Mike, Vinnie and Alice sell too, driving Monero lower still.

One thing the people mentioned above have in common is that *they're human*. Humans are emotional, which is why trend investing can work. The hard part is, of course, spotting the trend early enough to make a profit.

That's where TA can help.

One of the easiest and most effective ways to spot trends is the **Simple Moving Average**.

Simple Moving Average

The **Simple Moving Average (SMA)** is just what it sounds like: a *moving* average. The 50-day SMA, for example, is the average price over the last 50 days. Tomorrow, it would also be the average price over the last 50 days. Hence it is a moving average.

The next chart shows the Iota price (the black line) compared to its 50-day SMA (the grey line):

Iota price vs. 50-day SMA (Nov/Dec 2017)

Per the above, you can use the SMA to show whether the trend is up or down. You can then buy or sell cryptos (or stocks, gold, whatever you like) based on that trend:

- **Buy signal**: when the iota price rises *above* the 50-day SMA, it signals an uptrend (bullish).

- **Sell signal**: when it drops *below* the 50-day SMA, it signals a downtrend (bearish).

SMA's come in many sizes: 50-day, 30-day, 20-day, 13-day and 5-day are common for cryptos. Longer-day SMA's often have more predictive power than shorter-day SMA's.

Golden cross vs. death cross

How different SMA's cross each other can also have predictive power:

- **Golden cross**: a short-term SMA rises above a longer-term SMA. This is a **buy signal**.

- **Death cross**: a short-term SMA drops below a longer-term SMA. This is a **sell signal**.

Golden cross and Death cross: Litecoin (Dec 2017)

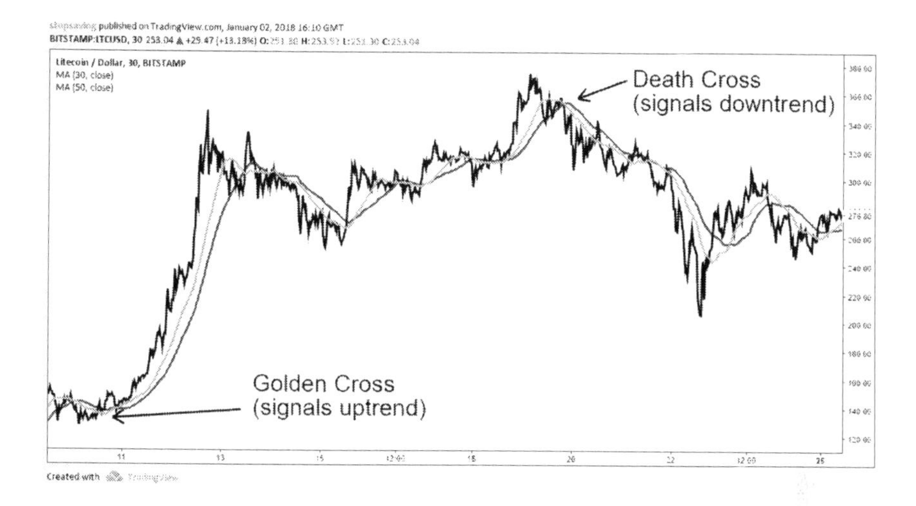

In the chart above, the dark grey line is the 50-day SMA, the light grey line is the 30-day SMA, and the black line is the price of Litecoin in USD. The two points that are labelled on the graph show where each cross is formed.

Trend lines

The price of a coin might go all over the place in the short-term, but there could be a strong trend in the longer term. **Trend lines** are used to spot these trends by cutting out the short-term noise.

To find trends using trend lines, look at the highs and lows of a chart over a space of time...

Trend lines: Neo (Oct/Nov 2017)

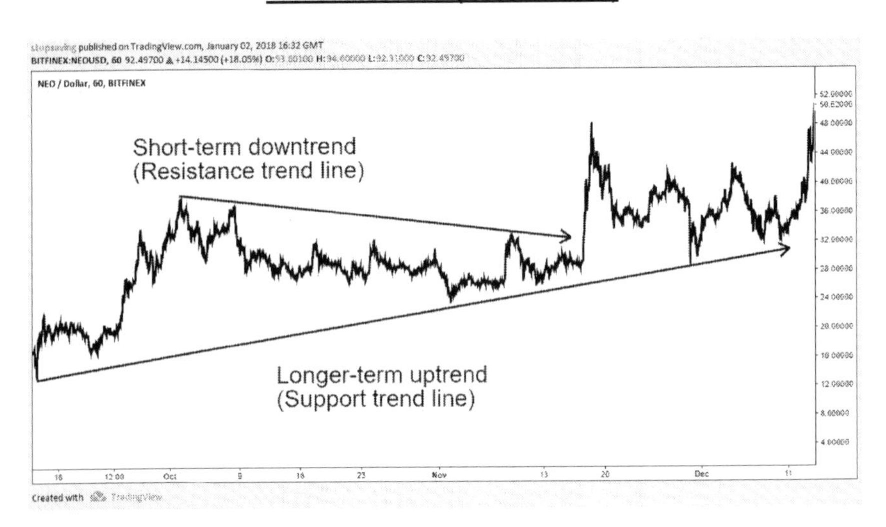

The above chart shows two trend lines for NEO:

- **Short-term downtrend**: also known as a **resistance trend**. Each high point is a resistance level on the price. As the resistance levels go down, they put downward pressure on the price.

- **Longer-term uptrend**: also known as a **support trend**. Each low point is a **support level** for the price. As the support levels rise, the trend goes up.

Trends can be sideways too if they have no clear up or down direction. When this happens, you can still make money trading in and out of the trend.

A short-term Value Averaging trading strategy, for example, would mean you buy more coins below the trend line and fewer above it, and sell coins if you get a short-term upward spike. In this case, you would trade when the 'chart looks good', rather than wait a month between trades as you would with the CP strategy.

Short-term trading strategies like the one I've just described can be effective, but you need to know exactly what you're doing. If you don't, you'll get wiped out and be stressed out the whole time. If short-term trading is something you want to learn, only start with very small amounts of money to build your skills before you start trading 'for real'.

Trend reversals

Spotting **trend reversals** (when a trend changes) is just as important as spotting trends. If you can consistently get these right, you could make decent profits. But this much easier said than done.

One way to potentially spot a trend reversal is when a short-term moving average crosses a longer-term one - we discussed this a few pages ago with the *golden cross* and the *death cross*.

Another is by playing *Chart Pictionary*...

Chart Pictionary and TA

Head and shoulders, *reverse head and shoulders*, *double bottoms*, *double tops*, *triple bottoms* and *triple tops* are all trading terms for types of chart patterns (or pictures) that signal the potential change of a trend. They are based on **support** and **resistance levels.**

- **A support level supports the price from falling.** The more times the price bounces back up from the support level, the stronger the support becomes, and the more likely it is that the trend will change from down to up.

- **A resistance level resists the price from rising.** The more times the price bounces back down from the resistance level, the stronger the resistance becomes, and the more likely it is that the trend will change from up to down.

These types of pictures are fairly easy to spot on a price chart. On the next page, you can see a few of them with Stratis:

Chart reversal patterns: Stratis (2017)

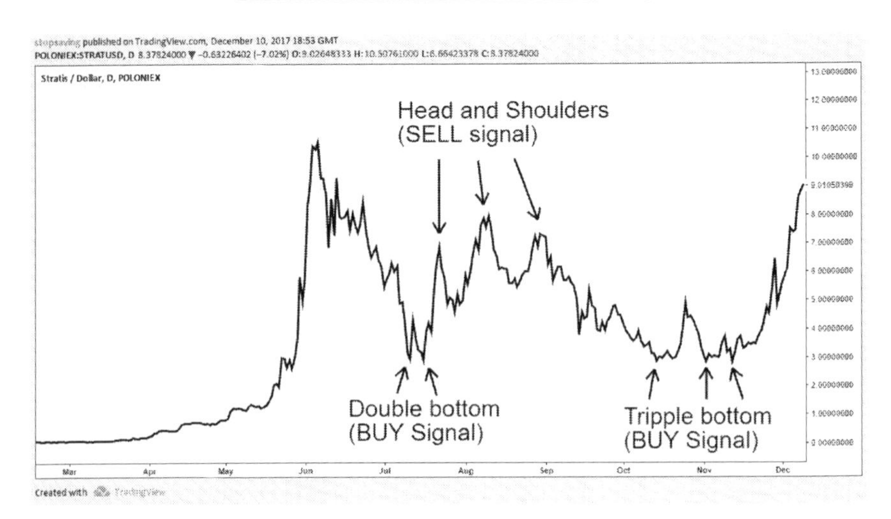

Bollinger bands

John Bollinger invented Bollinger bands in the 1980s[62] to spot trends by looking at both volatility and price. An **upper Bollinger band** and a **lower one** are plotted on either side of the price line. Most of the time, the price moves up and down within the range of the upper and lower bands. When it moves out of the range, it can signal the change of a trend.

Let me explain this on the next page using the price chart for Dash as an example...

Bollinger bands: Dash (Nov/Dec 2017)

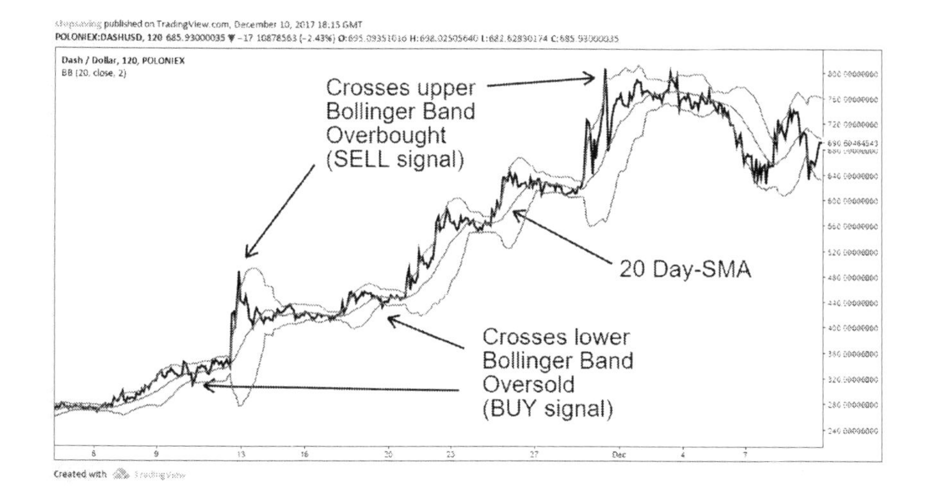

The above picture has a few things going on when it comes to Bollinger bands:

- The grey line in the middle of the two bands is the **20-Day SMA**. This shows the general direction of the trend.

- **The distance between the upper and lower bands** shows the **volatility** of Dash. When the bands are far apart, the Dash price line (black) is more volatile (bumpier). When the bands are close together, the price is less volatile (the black line is less bumpy).

- **When the price line crosses the upper Bollinger band**, this could be a sign that Dash is *overbought*. In other words, lots of Dash has been bought already, so there isn't much left to buy. This means the trend could be changing from up to down, so it's time to *sell*.

- **When the price line crosses the lower band**, this could be a sign that Dash is *oversold*, meaning there isn't much Dash left to sell. This is interpreted as a *buy signal*, as the trend could be changing from down to up.

Relative Strength Indicator (RSI)

Like Bollinger bands, the **Relative Strength Indicator (RSI)** can be used to show whether an investment is overbought (sell signal) or oversold (buy signal).

The RSI is a number between 1 and 100:

- **An RSI above 70** shows that the investment is overbought. This is a sell signal.

- **An RSI below 30** shows that the investment is oversold. This is a buy signal.

The box below explains the maths behind the RSI:

RSI maths

The RSI a number between 1 and 100 that is calculated with a formula developed by Welles Wilder[63]:

RSI = 100 – (100 / (1 +RS))

Where...

RS = (Av. Gain of Up Periods over each of the last 14 days) /
(Av. Loss of Down Periods over each of the last 14 days)

14 Days is the default number of days in the above equation, but 21 days is also common. Here's how we can interpret the maths...

1. **Starting with RS**: if the top part of the equation is bigger than the bottom part, this means that, on average, the gains of each 'up period' are greater than the losses of each 'down period'.

2. The more the top part of the equation 'wins' over the bottom part, the higher the value for RS.

3. **RSI**: if we plug in a higher value for RS into the RSI equation, then the inside bracket (1 + RS) gets bigger too.

4. If (1 + RS) gets bigger, then 100 / (1 + RS) gets smaller. When that happens, the RSI gets closer to 100.

5. **The closer the RSI is to 100**, the more the average gains are winning over the average losses. In other words, the more overbought the investment is, and the more chance the uptrend could change to a downtrend.

6. **Oppositely, the closer the RSI is to zero**, the more the average gains are losing to the average losses. Or, the more oversold the investment. This gives a greater chance of the downtrend reversing into an uptrend.

7. As it turns out, an RSI value above 70 suggests an overbought market (sell signal). A value below 30 shows an oversold market (buy signal).

The chart below shows the 14-day RSI for Zcash (in USD):

Relative Strength Indicator: Zcash (Nov/Dec 2017)

In this book, we only cover some of the TA basics. There are many other more complex indicators such as Fibonacci retracements (Fib), Moving Average Convergence Divergence (MACD), Exponential Moving Averages (EMA) and so on. These are all used to spot trends or trend reversals to make it easier for traders to know when to buy or sell. I'll be writing more about TA on ***www.stopsaving.com****.*

Using TA in your investment strategy

TA works better when lots of indicators say the same thing. For example, if the RSI and Bollinger Bands both say Bitcoin Cash is oversold, and it just so happens the chart is double bottoming, then there are more reasons to buy Bitcoin Cash. It's never a sure thing, but it's a whole lot better than guessing!

After some practice, you can start using TA to better time your crypto trades (when to buy and sell), which could improve your investment returns and limit your risk. But there are no guarantees.

Before investing any money using TA, you should first get comfortable reading the charts so you know how to spot and interpret different TA indicators. Cryptocompare.com and tradingview.com both offer great free charting software. It may help finding a YouTube video to get to grips with each of these charting tools faster.

Once you're up to speed with charting software and interpreting different TA indicators, you can then start investing with very small amounts of money, until you build the skills to take things further.

Chapter Summary

1. *Technical Analysis (TA) is when you look at past price and volume patterns in charts to try and predict what's going to happen next. This helps you decide whether to buy or sell.*

2. *The Simple Moving Average (SMA) is a moving average of the prices over the last X number of days. It gives a smoother line than the price line. It's a buy signal if the price line moves above the SMA line, and a sell signal if it moves below it.*

3. *A Golden Cross (buy signal) is when a shorter-day SMA crosses above a longer-day SMA from below. A Death cross (sell signal) is when a shorter-day SMA crosses below a longer-day SMA from above.*

4. *Trend lines are another way to spot price trends. A support trend (buy signal) is when the lows get higher. A resistance trend (sell signal) is when the highs get lower.*

5. *Double and triple bottom patterns (buy signals) spot potential trend reversals from down to up. Head and shoulders patterns do the opposite.*

6. *Bollinger bands and the Relative Strength Indicator (RSI) look at trading volume to try and predict trend reversals.*

7. *TA doesn't always work. If you are going to use TA, make sure it's with a very small amount of money, until you get better at it.*

CHAPTER 20

INITIAL COIN OFFERINGS

"It used to be that you had to come to Silicon Valley, walk up Sand Hill Road, network with individuals. That's now being completely changed and turned on its head by the whole ICO thing."

Balaji S. Srinivasan

Satoshi Nakomoto started Bitcoin with an email to some of his peers. From there, Bitcoin got big. These days, most new crypto coins start out with **Initial Coin Offerings (ICOs)**.

What are ICOs?

ICOs are the crypto version of crowdfunding. The crowd (people like you and me) send ether, bitcoin or some other type of payment to a team of developers who need money to launch a new crypto project.

In exchange for the money they invest in the ICO, the crowd receive **crypto tokens** for the project at a very low price - before other people can buy them on crypto exchanges. Later, when the tokens list on an exchange, the crowd can sell them at a potentially higher price or hold them as longer-term investments.

The next example explains the basic structure of an ICO deal in more detail. This is an extensive example that will give you a basic understanding of how ICOs work.

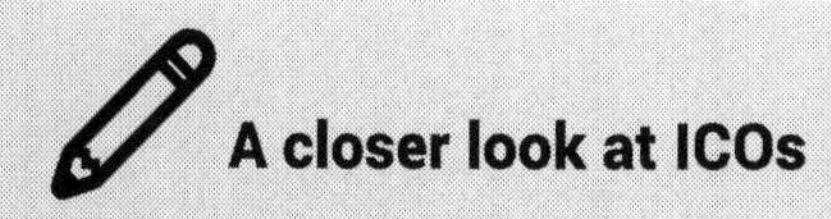

A closer look at ICOs

Michelle is the CEO of a new crypto project called **Exchange Token (ET)**. She has a strong team of developers, partners and advisers working with her to help make ET a success.

The ET system works like this:

1. ET is an **exchange** where people can buy and sell cryptos.
2. If people buy other cryptos with **Exchange Tokens (Ets)** on the ET exchange, they pay lower trading costs than if they use other coins like ether or bitcoin.
3. Et holders also get monthly 'Et dividends' for investing in Ets. These are paid out to investors as part of the profits made on the ET exchange.

Everything is programmed with smart contracts. All details of the project and the ICO are covered in the **ET whitepaper**, which investors can download on the ET website.

ET ICO funding needs

For ET to prosper, Michelle and her team want **10,000 ether (ETH)** to grow the project, which they will split like this:

Money	What they want it for
6,000 ETH	Pay developers to improve the ET platform.
3,000 ETH	Marketing and promotion to get people to use the ET exchange.
1,000 ETH	Legal and admin costs of the ICO.

They also want another **10,000 ETH** to pay the people who helped build ET from the ground up:

Money	What they want it for
4,000 ETH	Pay Michelle and the other partners of ET.
3,000 ETH	Pay advisors for advice given during the ICO.
3,000 ETH	Pay early angel investors who supported the project from day one.

Finally, they need Ets to have a **starting value** so that people can use them to trade cryptos on the ET exchange. The team hope the value of Ets will go up after the ICO as more people buy the tokens.

The ET team would, therefore, like to raise another **80,000 ETH** to give Ets a starting value.

To sum up, Michelle and her team want to raise **100,000 ETH** (roughly $50 million at the time) in total through the ICO crowdsale:

- 10,000 ETH to grow the project.
- 10,000 ETH for the founders, advisers and angel investors.
- 80,000 ETH to give the tokens a starting value.

ICO deal structure for investors

To raise the 100,000 ETH, the ET Team will issue **500 million Ets** to ICO investors. This is based on the exchange rate of 5,000 Ets per 1 ETH (or 10 cents per Et in dollars).

The team realize they might go above or below the 500 million Ets **target** depending on investor interest in the ICO crowdsale. In the whitepaper and on their website, they give more details:

Amount raised	Scenario
500 million Ets	**Target** if things go according to plan.
750 million Ets	**Hard cap**: if things go very well. This is the maximum amount they will raise. If they raise *more* than 750 million Ets, they will 'burn' the extra tokens (make them permanently worthless) that they don't need for the project. This is because they want to make sure the investors aren't wasting their money.
250 million Ets	**Soft cap**: the lowest amount of Ets they must raise to go ahead with the project.
Less than 250 million Ets	**Failure:** those who did invest will have their ETH returned to them and the ICO will not happen.

ICO Timeline

To buy Ets during the ICO crowdsale, investors must send ETH to the ET Ethereum address during the ICO. Below are the deadlines:

- **The ICO starts on December 1st** and is expected to last for two weeks unless the 750 million hard cap is reached before then.

  Investors who don't deposit ETH during that time can't take part in the ICO crowdsale.

- After investors make the ETH payment, their Ets are held in **escrow** (a trusted third party) until **December 25th**, when investors get their Ets for Christmas.

- On **January 15th**, Ets can be traded on the ET exchange for USD or other cryptos.

- On **January 30th**, Ets will also list on other crypto exchanges. The ET team rightfully do not disclose *which* exchanges will trade the tokens. This is to protect them from any potential legal issues around token price manipulation.

Investing in ICOs

If you do your homework, you can make a lot of money investing in ICOs. If you don't, you could lose every cent you put in. ICOs are the wild west of cryptos, which is saying a lot!

With ICOs, it's possible for project teams (or companies) to raise millions of dollars much faster and more easily than it is through traditional funding avenues, such as Venture Capital. This is good for the companies and entrepreneurs raising the money as well as for ordinary investors.

The average Joe on the street can now easily invest in promising startup projects through ICOs. In the past, these opportunities were only reserved for a privileged few.

That said, dangers of equal measure come with the territory. ICOs are a thinly regulated (if at all) way for companies to raise millions from unsuspecting investors. Like a moth to a flame, this has attracted all kinds of shady characters promoting useless 'scam coins' to make a quick buck.

In this chapter, we'll go through some steps to help you:

1. Filter out potential ICO scams and bad investments.

2. Find genuinely good ICO investment opportunities.

An entire thesis could be written about ICO investing. In this chapter, we'll just go over the basics. Before going ahead with any ICOs, make sure to do as much research as possible. Some of the extra resources at the end of this book can help with this.

ICO investment research and screening

Here are some things to consider when looking at a potential ICO investment:

1. **The Project Team**: a great team is paramount to the success of any business venture, including ICOs. If you're going trust them with your money, the CEO, founders, partners, developers and advisors should be a mix of entrepreneurial, business and crypto rock stars.

   Good teams:

   - Have **strong experience** that is *relevant* to the project.

   - Have worked at **reputable** companies before or have been involved in previously successful entrepreneurial ventures.

   - Are who they say they are.

   - Have **a lot to lose** if they break investor trust by scamming them.

- Are **easy to contact** via various social media outlets and by email.

To cover your bases, you can:

1. Google the team members.

2. Make sure their Linkedin profiles match up with who they say they are.

3. Make sure their Linkedin profiles say something about them being part of the ICO. If they don't, the 'ICO team' could be made up of fake or random people.

2. **Product and technology**: if the product doesn't have any real-world value, it's not worth your time. It's a good sign if the product:

- **Solves a real problem** in a unique and compelling way.

- Has a **prototype**. Or better yet, is already being used today. This makes it more than just an idea on a whitepaper (see point three on the next page).

- **Needs blockchain** or crypto technology to make it work. If it doesn't, the ICO team could just be trying to raise money for an idea that was already rejected through traditional funding, like Venture Capital.

- Has **first mover advantage.** The product could be great, but if there are already better products out there, it's harder for it to succeed.

  If the product doesn't have first mover advantage, then it must have a realistic chance of gaining market share from the first mover.

To research this:

1. Read the whitepaper on the ICO website in detail.

2. Watch any videos explaining how the technology works. These can be on the website itself or by third parties on YouTube (see extra resources section).

3. If you're technical, read the project source code on github.com. If the source code isn't on Github, the developers might have something to hide!

3. **Whitepaper**: this is the blueprint for the project that you can download from the ICO website. The whitepaper should be easy to understand, clearly written and well presented. It should also match up with what's on the project's website.

4. **Roadmap**: the whitepaper, website or both should explain the business model and give a detailed timeline of upcoming project targets. The roadmap should be realistic. If it looks too ambitious, it probably is.

5. **Token necessity**: if the token isn't needed to use the product, it's price could go down once it goes on an exchange. Think back to the *Exchange Token* example at the start of this chapter. Traders can still use the exchange without Ets, but the lower trading fees and Et dividends are good incentives to use the tokens.

6. **Token economics**: put on your value investor hat to decide whether the tokens are a good bargain. This takes serious analysis and you will only get better at it by reading and researching lots of different ICOs. Signs of good token economics are:

   - **The hard cap is low** for the project. If the team are raising less money, they are more likely to put it to good use because they will only have a limited amount of cash to work with. This also gives the market cap more potential room to grow after the ICO.

   - **Most of the tokens go to the ICO investors**. If the team are taking too big of a cut, that's a bad sign.

   - **Bounties, bonuses or discounts** for investing in the ICO early. This helps the team achieve their funding needs and can be good for investors at the same time, who may be awarded extra tokens or receive a discounted token price in the ICO.

- **Team and advisor reward tokens are vested.** With each ICO, some of the tokens raised go the team and their advisers to reward them for their work. This is obviously fair and encouraged. But what's to stop them from cashing out their tokens as soon as they raise the money? If their tokens are *vested*, they can't sell their tokens straight after the ICO by dumping them on the exchanges.

  This also means the team have more skin in the game because their future wealth depends on the growth of the token. It's a good sign if the team and advisor tokens are vested for at least a few years.

- **Maximum purchase limit for each investor.** This stops one investor buying too many tokens and then dumping them on the exchanges to crash the price.

- **Fixed supply of total tokens:** a fixed supply means long-term scarcity. If the token is scarce, it's price could go up as more people demand the token.

Token economics is technical. Comparing lots of different ICOs will help give you a feel for what's fair and what isn't!

7. **Know Your Customer (KYC) requirements:** just like with crypto exchanges, the more KYC hoops you must jump through, the better. If you need to upload a photo of you with your passport to take part in the ICO, that's a good thing. This helps stop potential money laundering.

8. **Hype, ratings and market opinion:** these can all have a big impact on the price of the token once it lists on the exchange. Some things to look out for include:

- **ICO Telegram Chat status**: Telegram Messenger is a social media tool where thousands of people can join the same chat group.

  ICO teams use Telegram to make announcements leading up to, during, and after each ICO. If the ICO chat group has thousands of people on it, that's a strong indication of market interest in the project.

  Always sign up to the Telegram chat of any ICO you are considering investing in. Scroll through the comments in the chats from the members to help assess the hype of the ICO in question. Also, see how the team responds to questions from chat members to gauge the team's efficiency and credibility. *Never* send cryptos to an address that appears on the Telegram chat as they are easy targets for scammers impersonating team members.

- **Public appearances**: it's a bonus if the CEO of the project appears on Bloomberg, Yahoo Finance, CNBC or any other mainstream financial media outlet. It's a bigger bonus if they confidently and concisely answer every question the show presenter asks them.

- **Crypto forum comments**: see what people are saying about the ICO on Reddit, bitcointalk.org and CryptoCompare forums. As with all crypto forums, sometimes people try to 'pump the ICO' with false news, so always research the validity of the comments online if things sound too good to be true. This applies to all cryptos, not just ICOs!

- **Reviews by ICO authorities**: there are blogs, websites and YouTube channels dedicated to researching and reviewing ICOs. These reviews can have a big impact on the hype of the ICO. Of course, some review services are better than others. I've included what I think are the best in the extra resources section at the end of this book.

- **Name**: it might sound silly, but a good name can add huge hype to an ICO and a cryptocurrency. Neo, Next, Ethereum, Stratis, Golem and Waves all have great names (in my opinion) and their ICOs did rather well.

Quick ways of spotting the scams:

As mentioned before, ICOs aren't regulated in the same way as traditional investments, so they are appealing to scammers. At the same time, many project teams are genuinely trying to start a business and improve the world with new and exciting crypto-based technologies.

As the ICO market matures, it is likely to become much more heavily regulated. But for now, you need to do your own regulation to sniff out the scams. The ICO investment screening process I described above can help with this - although there are no guarantees.

Apart from that, the following red flags should at once set off your ICO scam detector:

1. **The project promises or 'guarantees' returns to investors**. if it sounds too good to be true, it's a lie!

2. **Careless typos or poor grammar on the website and whitepaper**: this suggests the ICO marketing was hurried.

3. **No online presence of the team members**: if you can't find them on Google or Linked in, they probably don't exist.

Strategy for ICO investing:

The first and most important thing with ICO investing is that you research the project as much as you can. If after that you're happy investing in the ICO, you can then take further steps to help reduce the risks:

1. **Only invest money you can afford to lose**: this goes without saying. Here's why you should only invest a very small amount of money into a single ICO:

    - No matter how much research you do, there is still a chance the ICO could tank miserably, meaning you could lose most if not all of your investment.

- There are no guarantees, but good ICOs could earn you up to five or even ten times your original investment, so you don't *need* to invest a lot up front.

Using data from icostats.com and coinmarketcap.com, the next table shows the percentage returns you would have earned if you had invested $10 in some of the best performing ICOs of the past. This assumes you bought in at the ICO price and held the investment until the end of December 2017:

ICO	ICO date (d/m/y)	ICO Coin price ($)	Coin Price ($) 31st Dec 2017	Value of $10 invested
Next	28/09/13	0.000168	0.7059	42,020
Ethereum	22/07/14	0.0311	756.73	243,322
Neo	01/10/15	0.032	75.96	23,738
IOTA	25/11/15	0.000435	3.55	81,701
Lisk	22/02/16	0.076	20.41	2,686
Waves	12/04/16	0.188	12.60	670
Stratis	20/06/16	0.007	14.03	20,043
QTUM	12/03/17	0.292	62.40	2,137
Populus	24/06/17	0.278	41.53	1,494
Omisego	15/07/17	0.244	19.89	815

The above numbers are just for illustration and are not meant to be taken as a suggestion that you should invest in ICOs. Most ICOs don't do anywhere near as well as these. As always, past performance is no guide to future returns.

2. **Spread your ICO bets with the *venture capital approach***: venture capital (VC) funds invest in lots of different startup projects at once. They know that many might fail, but only need some of them to reach their full potential for the VC fund to do well.

   For example, if you have £500 to invest in ICOs, it's less risky putting £50 in ten different ICOs then going all in on just one. If only three good ICOs are happening at the same time, you would just invest £150 in total (or £50 in each of the three ICOs) and wait until better opportunities come up before investing the remaining £350.

3. **Take a small amount of profit (if there are profits) shortly after the ICO tokens hit the exchanges**: a common strategy amongst ICO investors is to get in and get out as soon as they can. This is because, very often, the price of the token peaks shortly after it first lists on the exchange and never reaches new highs.

   That said, you shouldn't invest in an ICO just because you think the price will pump straight after it lists on an exchange. Instead, you should invest in it because you think the project has good long-term value. However, even if you believe in the long-term value of the token, you could still sell a small portion of your tokens if the price pumps soon after it lists on the exchange. You can assess this case by case for each ICO.

   The graph below (source cryptocompare.com)[64] shows the performance of EOS versus bitcoin since its ICO on July 26th, 2017. Soon after EOS started trading on Bitfinex[65], its price rose through the roof. Taking some profits here (by selling *some* EOS for bitcoin, for example) would have been a good call.

   Any yet, EOS is now ranked 12th on Coinmarketcap.com as I write this, and it could turn out to be a good long-term investment. Keeping some of the cheaply bought ICO tokens for a few years would also be sensible in this case.

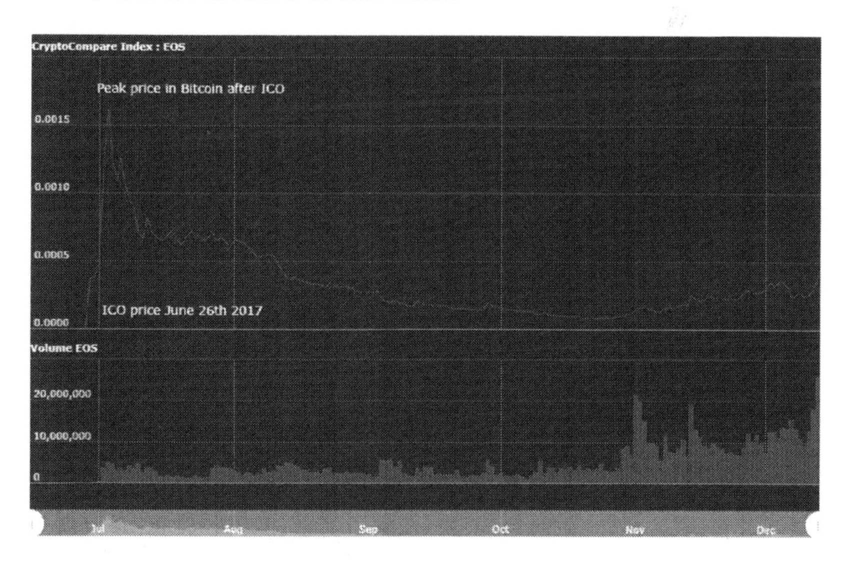

The chart on the last page is priced in bitcoin. In USD, the price of EOS has gone from $0.925 at ICO to around $9 at the end of December 2017.

As a side note, the price of new tokens can increase each time the token is listed on a new exchange, so pay attention to the Telegram Channel to stay updated on new exchange listings.

If you are awarded **bonus tokens** in the ICO, it's often the case that you receive them after the tokens you paid for are already listed on the exchange. A simple strategy here could be to:

- Sell some of the tokens you paid for if the price spikes soon after the ICO.

- Keep the bonus tokens (which were free) invested for the long-term.

4. **Factor in market sentiment for Ethereum**: these days, most ICOs want payment in ether. This means you sell ether for the ICO token. If ether is doing well at the time, other investors might prefer keeping their money in ether to investing in an ICO. This can reduce the overall success of the ICO as fewer people invest in it.

   Some ICOs also accept payment in other cryptocurrencies like bitcoin, litecoin or neo. The same logic applies here.

Process for ICO investing

The process of investing in an ICO can seem intimidating at first. In a nutshell, here are the usual steps you would take:

1. **Check if you can participate in the ICO** in your home country. You should be able to find this information on the ICO website.

2. **Sign up to the ICO 'whitelist'** as early as possible - *before* you have completed your research. This will ensure you can take part in the ICO if you later decide to invest in it. Sometimes, ICOs can

sell out quickly or even before the ICO date if the participants list closes to new investors.

You can usually get on the whitelist by entering your email address to a form on the ICO website. If you sign up early enough, there's a chance you could take part in the **pre-ICO** at an even lower price than the ICO price. But be warned, this can be riskier than ICO investing as there is usually less information to go on.

3. **Sign up to the ICO Telegram chat or announcement channel:** this way you stay updated on all things related to the ICO. For example, when the tokens will list on an exchange. You can also use the Telegram channel to question the ICO team members.

4. **Do the KYC early on:** if you do the KYC up front, you'll be ready to invest as soon as the ICO goes live. KYC doesn't take long - you usually need to upload a photo of your passport or ID and a photo of you holding it to the ICO website.

5. **Deposit ether, neo or bitcoin to your cold wallet before you invest:** Regardless of which cryptocurrency you buy ICO tokens with, it must be sent from your cold wallet address.

To sum up

ICOs aren't for the fainted hearted. But if you do the research, you could potentially earn high returns on your investments. If you invest in ICOs, make sure it's with money you can afford to lose. In the future, ICO investing (or something similar) is likely to become more common and much better regulated. Understanding how ICOs work today could put you at a financial advantage further down the road.

 Chapter Summary

1. *ICOs are a way for companies and project teams to raise money from ordinary investors (people like you and me) so they can launch new crypto tokens.*

2. *In exchange for investing their money in ICOs, investors get tokens at a low price. If they can sell those tokens later at a higher price on an exchange, investors can make money.*

3. *If you know what you're doing, you can make a lot of money with ICOs. You can lose a lot of money if you don't.*

4. *When researching potential ICO investments, your first job is to filter out the scams. Next, look for projects with good long-term growth potential. The more research you do, the better.*

5. *Use the venture capital approach when investing in ICOs. This means investing small amounts in different ICOs, rather than a large amount in just one.*

6. *The best ICOs often sell out fast, so get on the whitelist and send your KYC early on to secure your place in the ICO. You can always change your mind later and decide not to invest.*

CHAPTER 21

INVESTING IN UNDERVALUED COINS

"Buy low and sell high. It's pretty simple. The problem is knowing what's low and what's high."

Jim Rogers

In the world of cryptocurrencies, you often hear about people making overnight fortunes with 'unknown' coins by investing in them before the herd. By the time the coins *moon*, they are the topics of every crypto chat forum, as FOMO kicks in. Frantically, more people read about the 'new' coin online, buy as much of it as they can, tell their friends, post about it on Facebook and, before you know it, the coin is featured on mainstream media as "the next bitcoin".

Then the price crashes 25% in a day.

People panic sell. The price goes down more over the next few weeks. The FOMO investors lose a lot of money. But the investors who got in cheap and early are still up hundreds of percent.

Unfortunately, crypto newbies fall for this trick all the time. But as they gain experience, they learn that FOMO doesn't pay.

The CP strategy covered in part two of this book is one way to stop you from falling for the FOMO trap. You choose ten coins at the start of each year and invest in them with Value Averaging each month. The coins have large market caps and are already well established in the crypto market, so you don't need to worry about a new coin coming along to steal the FOMO show. Next year, if that new coin is consistently doing well, you can include it in your next CP.

The difference between value and price

Another way to cure FOMO is to buy coins before the hype. This is easier said than done, but with enough research, you could find bargain crypto investments - or **undervalued coins.**

The price of a coin at any point in time is what investors are willing to pay for it on an exchange. But when it comes to investing, price and value are two different things.

- An **undervalued** coin is priced lower than its true value. This means the crypto market is *underestimating* its potential to grow in the long-term.

- An **overvalued** coin is priced higher than its true value. Because of all the FOMO, its price has been driven much higher than it should be. The crypto market is *overestimating* its potential to grow in the long-term.

Cryptos are a new asset class. Unlike stocks or bonds, for example, we don't yet have established financial models to approximate their real values. I'm sure we will one day, but in the meantime, we need to look at the value of a coin relative to other coins in the crypto market.

There are no guarantees, but undervalued coins could be safer investments than overvalued ones. If a coin is overvalued, its price could drop by much more than the price of an undervalued coin, which is already low.

Efficient Market Hypothesis

The **efficient market hypothesis (EMH)** is a well-known theory in the stock market:

If a stock market (like the S&P500 for example) is very well developed, you have a research overload for all its stocks. Since every stock in the market is researched by lots of different investors, the stock prices and their true values become fairly similar. Because of this, many financial advisers suggest investing in index tracker funds that match the performance of the stock market, rather than trying to beat it.

Not everyone agrees with the EMH. I for one know of several active fund managers who beat the stock market consistently by choosing undervalued stocks[7].

However, there is some degree of truth in the EMH. The less efficient (less developed) the stock market, the easier it is to find undervalued stocks. We know this because active fund managers have a better track record of beating index tracker funds in emerging (less developed) stock markets than they do in developed stock markets[66].

Put another way, there's more chance of good investment research paying off in less developed markets.

Since the crypto market is still so new, its far less developed than most stock markets. Therefore, the right research could potentially pay off big in the long run.

[7] For more on mutual fund investing, read my other book, *Stop Saving Start Investing: Ten Simple Rules for Effectively Investing in Funds.*

How to find undervalued coins

The *theory* of **value investing** is straightforward:

1. Do the research. The more research you do, the better.

2. Find an investment that is selling at a bargain - where its price is lower than what your research suggests it should really be worth.

3. Buy the investment and hold it until lots of other investors notice the investment's true value and start buying it for themselves.

4. Sell the investment when the price looks too high - once the investment is selling at a price that is higher than its true value.

With cryptos, value investing is difficult as you first need to find the value of a coin - what you think it should really be worth in the market. This is more of an art than a science, and you will never get it exactly right.

However, you can use some of the points from the last chapter about ICO investing to help you decide if the coin is a bargain investment or a rip-off. Look out for:

1. **A good development team** with strong leadership, and team members with good track records of past successes - especially if they involve crypto technology.

2. **A great product** that solves a real-world problem using crypto technology. Find a coin that has utility and is *needed* to make the project work.

3. **A coin that does something unique** for the first time, or is doing something that is already being done in a better way than the competition.

4. **Partnerships with global companies**, who have a lot to lose if those partnerships don't succeed.

5. **More than just a whitepaper**: if there is only a whitepaper and no actual functioning product, then the hype is the only thing driving the price.

6. **An achievable roadmap**: if the crypto is trying to do too much, it's unlikely to achieve all its goals. Look for something achievable. This way, if the coin achieves what the team sets out to do, other investors will begin to trust the project.

Next, look for things to do with the price of the coin:

7. If the price has already gone up hundreds of percent in a month, find out why. If it looks like hype, it probably is.

8. If there are other coins that do similar things but have higher market caps than the coin you are researching, again find out why. If you can't find a reason, the coin could be undervalued.

9. What does the coin's price chart look like? Use Technical Analysis to look for gradual longer-term uptrends. This could be a sign that investors are buying the coin to hold it long term because they believe it to be undervalued.

10. Does the price crash when the market crashes? If the entire crypto market goes down 15% in a day (this happens often), does the coin you are researching go down by more or less than 15%? If it goes down by less, it could be a sign that there are investors who don't want to sell. Again, they may not want to sell because they see long-term value in the coin.

To conclude

Finding undervalued coins takes time and effort, but you could be well rewarded for it. Of course, if you do find an undervalued coin, there are no guarantees that its price will catch up to its value. And if the price does catch up, it may take a while. Therefore, as with all investments, patience is key.

It's also a good idea to have a portfolio of perhaps ten undervalued coins, rather than just a few. As with ICOs, you only need one or two of them to reach their full potential for your portfolio to do well.

I hope this part of the book has given you some options to take your crypto investing further. Technical Analysis, ICOs and finding undervalued coins all take a long time to master, so don't expect results straight away. If you do wish to explore any of these strategies, it goes without saying that you should start small, with money you can afford to lose, until you build the skills to take things further.

I would also encourage you to spend a bit of time each day learning more about cryptocurrencies and crypto investing strategies. To help with this, I've included some extra resources after the next (and final) chapter of this book.

Chapter Summary

1. *FOMO is a terrible investment strategy. It's far better to research coins with good fundamentals and buy them when prices are low. This is easier said than done.*

2. *An undervalued coin is priced lower than its true value. This means the crypto market is underestimating its potential to grow in the long term.*

3. *An overvalued coin is priced higher than its true value; its price has been hyped much higher than it should be. The crypto market is overestimating its potential to grow in the long term.*

4. *The crypto market is new, so it isn't as well researched as most stock markets. This means there could be more opportunities for good research to pay off. Put another way, with good research, you stand a good chance of beating the returns of the crypto market as a whole.*

CHAPTER 22

WHAT'S NEXT?

The tortoise is patient and knows that the race is long.

I am sure you know the story of the tortoise and the hare. The hare may be the faster animal, but the tortoise wins the race in the end. This is because the tortoise doesn't give up and focuses on the end goal. The hare, on the other hand, sprints ahead, before falling asleep under a tree.

When investing in anything, always be the tortoise in this analogy. Try to earn slow, steady returns while managing your investment risks. Don't try to sprint ahead and get rich quick – this usually ends badly.

Cryptocurrencies are a new type of investment, but the old rules of commonsense investing still apply. Regardless of which investment strategy you use, make sure your emotions don't get in the way. Be patient, do the research, stick to your strategy and watch your financial situation improve with time.

And if you lose money investing in cryptos, use that to your advantage. The knowledge you gain from losing money could pay off further on in your investment journey – crypto or otherwise. Besides, I hope you won't be investing too much into cryptos in the first place. This way if you do lose, you'll still be OK.

Where blockchain and cryptocurrencies go from here is anyone's guess, but I for one am excited about what the future holds. There will be bumps along the way I'm sure, but if crypto technology is half as revolutionary as it promises to be, tomorrow's world could be a better place for all. And if we can potentially earn a bit of extra money investing in *cryptos* along the way, well, that's OK too!

My sincere thanks for reading this far. I hope you enjoyed reading this book as much as I enjoyed writing it, and that you walk away with some practical knowledge which you can immediately put to good use. If you want to continue learning more about investing (crypto or otherwise), please have a look at the resources up next.

The end.

EXTRA RESOURCES

This book has given you a solid introduction to cryptocurrency investing. At the same time, there's always more to learn! To that end, I've included some extra resources below:

STOPSAVING.COM

Stopsaving.com is a blog I started in 2017. It covers a wide range of investment areas without all the financial mumbo-jumbo. If you want to know more about investing in funds, shares, bonds, cryptocurrencies, gold and more, then check it out!

There are also free spreadsheets to download from the blog to help with things like value averaging, dividend reinvesting, and calculating future value investment values based on desired investment returns.

In September 2017, I started a six-month Crypto Portfolio (following the CP strategy) with some of my own money to test the strategy while writing this book. I've put up a series of blog posts updating the progress of the portfolio here:

www.stopsaving.com/blog/my-crypto-investing-strategy.

Unfortunately, this book would be way too long if I covered more cryptocurrencies, so I plan on adding new posts about different coins in 2018 and beyond. You can visit the link below for more updates:

Website: www.stopsaving.com

COINTELEGRAPH.COM

Cointelegraph.com is a free news service for daily updates on all things cryptocurrency. The articles are informative and to the point. Reading a few articles each week will go a long way towards improving your knowledge of the crypto market.

Website: www.cointelgraph.com

OHHEYMATTY (YouTube channel)

OhHeyMatty's Youtube channel is as great resource for ICO investing. Using his background as a computer scientist and skills as a professional poker player, he takes his time going over different ICOs in detail, carefully weighing up the pros and cons of each investment.

As Matty says on his channel, the information he provides is not investment advice, and he encourages people to do their own research before investing in any ICO.

Even if you're not thinking about investing in ICOs, the channel is a great way to learn more about the fundamentals of different cryptocurrency projects.

Website: www.youtube.com/watch?v=GOxp1NIo1GI

CRYPTOCOMPARE.COM

As covered in chapter 17, cryptocompare.com has a plethora of features for crypto investors.

Website: www.cryptocompare.com

IVAN ON TECH (Youtube Channel)

Ivan Liljeqvist is a Swedish software developer. In his videos, he explains blockchain and crypto technologies in very simple terms.

Website: http://ivanontech.com

OTHER RESOURCES TO LOOK AT

While researching for this book, I found the below websites particularly helpful in improving my understanding of cryptos and blockchain:

www.blockgeeks.com

www.bitcoinmagazine.com

www.coingecko.com

www.coinmarketcap.com

www.99bitcoins.com

www.coindesk.com

www.bitcoin.org

www.weusecoins.com

https://blog.ethereum.org

www.reddit.com/r/CryptoCurrency/

https://steemit.com/trending/cryptocurrency

GET IN TOUCH

I would really like to hear from you if you have any questions or feedback about this book, investing in cryptos or investing in general. To get in contact, you can email me at the below address:

My email: jon@stopsaving.com

If you enjoyed the book, please leave a quick review on Amazon. Reviews mean everything to independent authors.

If you didn't like the book or if something didn't make sense, email me to let me know why. One of the great things about being a self-published author is that I can use your feedback to make the book better for the next reader!

Want to learn about investing in funds?

Crypto investing is risky, so it always makes sense to diversify. Mutual funds are a great way to do this. If you enjoyed the book you've just read, you might enjoy this one too!

Stop Saving Start Investing: Ten Simple Rules for Effectively Investing in Funds.

Amazon link: http://azon.ly/GExM

REFERENCES

[1] Historyofbitcoin.org. (2009). *Bitcoin History: The Complete History of Bitcoin [Timeline].* [online] Available at: http://historyofbitcoin.org/ [Accessed 18 Dec. 2017].

[2] World Bank. (2017). *2 Billion: Number of Adults Worldwide Without Access to Formal Financial Services.* [online] Available at: http://www.worldbank.org/en/news/video/2016/03/10/2-billion-number-of-adults-worldwide-without-access-to-formal-financial-services [Accessed 23 Oct. 2017].

[3] Google Trends. (2018). *Google's Year in Search.* [online] Available at: https://trends.google.com/trends/yis/2017/GLOBAL/ [Accessed 05 Jan. 2018].

[4] Cointelegraph. (2017). *First Bitcoin-Only Real Estate Transaction Completed in Texas.* [online] Available at: https://cointelegraph.com/news/first-bitcoin-only-real-estate-transaction-completed-in-texas [Accessed 01 Oct. 2017].

[5] McLeod, D. (2017). *Bitcoin now accepted at Pick n Pay.* [online] Moneyweb. Available at: https://www.moneyweb.co.za/news/tech/bitcoin-now-accepted-at-pick-n-pay/ [Accessed 01 Oct. 2017].

[6] Sky News. (2017). *From two pizzas to a £17m mansion: Bubble fears over Bitcoin's soaring value.* [online] Available at: https://news.sky.com/story/from-two-pizzas-to-a-17m-mansion-bubble-fears-over-bitcoins-soaring-value-11090760 [Accessed 01 Oct. 2017].

[7] En.wikipedia.org. (2017). *Secure Hash Algorithms.* [online] Available at: https://en.wikipedia.org/wiki/Secure_Hash_Algorithms [Accessed 28 Nov. 2017].

[8] En.bitcoin.it. (2017). *Controlled supply - Bitcoin Wiki.* [online] Available at: https://en.bitcoin.it/wiki/Controlled_supply#Projected_Bitcoins_Long_Term [Accessed 28 Nov. 2017].

[9] Blockchain.info. (2017). *Hashrate Distribution.* [online] Available at: https://blockchain.info/pools [Accessed 05 Dec. 2017].

[10] Bevand, M. and Bevand, M. (2017). *Op Ed: Bitcoin Miners Consume A Reasonable Amount of Energy.* [online] Bitcoin Magazine. Available at: https://bitcoinmagazine.com/articles/op-ed-bitcoin-miners-consume-reasonable-amount-energy-and-its-all-worth-it/ [Accessed 05 Dec. 2017].

[11] Data Center Knowledge. (2017). *Google Data Center FAQ Part 3*. [online] Available at: http://www.datacenterknowledge.com/data-center-faqs/google-data-center-faq-part-3 [Accessed 18 Oct. 2017].

[12] CoinDesk. (2014). *Under the Microscope: The Real Costs of a Dollar*. [online] Available at: https://www.coindesk.com/microscope-real-costs-dollar/ [Accessed 18 Oct. 2017].

[13] CoinDesk. (2014). *Under the Microscope: The True Costs of Gold Production*. [online] Available at: https://www.coindesk.com/microscope-true-costs-gold-production/ [Accessed 18 Oct. 2017].

[14] Lee, T. (2017). *Bitcoin fees are skyrocketing*. [online] Ars Technica. Available at: https://arstechnica.com/tech-policy/2017/12/bitcoin-fees-are-skyrocketing/ [Accessed 18 Jan. 2018].

[15]Blockchain.info. (2017). *Transaction Rate*. [online] Available at: https://blockchain.info/charts/transactions-per-second?daysAverageString=7×pan=1year [Accessed 05 Jan. 2018].

[16]Usa.visa.com. (2018). *Visa acceptance for retailers*. [online] Available at: https://usa.visa.com/run-your-business/small-business-tools/retail.html [Accessed 05 Jan. 2018].

[17] Ferriss, T. (2017). *The Quiet Master of Cryptocurrency — Nick Szabo*. [online] The Blog of Author Tim Ferriss. Available at: https://tim.blog/2017/06/04/nick-szabo/ [Accessed 14 Nov. 2017].

[18] Google Docs. (2017). *Creating Litecoin 3/31/2017*. [online] Available at: https://bit.ly/coinbaseltc [Accessed 14 Nov. 2017].

[19] Google Docs. (2017). *Creating Litecoin 3/31/2017*. [online] Available at: https://bit.ly/coinbaseltc [Accessed 14 Nov. 2017].

[20] Coinist.io. (2017). *Beginners Guide to DASH*. [online] Available at: https://www.coinist.io/beginners-guide-to-dash [Accessed 14 Nov. 2017].

[21] Dash.org. (2018). *— Dash*. [online] Available at: https://www.dash.org/masternodes2/ [Accessed 15 Jan. 2018].

[22] Dash.org. (2017). *Dash Official Website | Dash Crypto Currency — Dash*. [online] Available at: https://www.dash.org/governance/ [Accessed 15 Jan. 2018].

[23] Bitcointalk.org. (2014). *[ANN][BMR] Bitmonero - a new coin based on*

CryptoNote technology - LAUNCHED. [online] Available at: https://bitcointalk.org/index.php?topic=563821.0 [Accessed 5 Nov. 2017].

[24] YouTube. (2017). *Ripple CEO interviewed at Bloomberg*. [online] Available at: https://www.youtube.com/watch?v=vsEVF4LV_gI [Accessed 5 Nov. 2017].

[25] CoinDesk. (2014). *Ripple Explained: Medieval Banking with a Digital Twist*. [online] Available at: https://www.coindesk.com/ripple-medieval-banking-digital-twist/ [Accessed 5 Nov. 2017].

[26] Anon, (2017). [online] Available at: https://www.quora.com/Why-is-Ripple-holding-50-billion-XRP [Accessed 11 Nov. 2017].

[27] Ripple. (2017). *Ripple - One Frictionless Experience to Send Money Globally | Ripple*. [online] Available at: https://ripple.com/ [Accessed 11 Nov. 2017].

[28] En.wikipedia.org. (2018). *Ethereum*. [online] Available at: https://en.wikipedia.org/wiki/Ethereum [Accessed 18 Jan. 2018].

[29] Buterin, V. (2018). *Vitalik Buterin on about.me*. [online] about.me. Available at: https://about.me/vitalik_buterin [Accessed 18 Jan. 2018].

[30] Anon, (2018). [online] Available at: https://etherscan.io/chart/blocktime [Accessed 18 Jan. 2018].

[31] Anon, (2018). [online] Available at: https://etherscan.io/chart/ethersupplygrowth [Accessed 18 Jan. 2018].

[32]Blockgeeks. (2017). *What is Ethereum Casper Protocol? Crash Course*. [online] Available at: https://blockgeeks.com/guides/ethereum-casper/ [Accessed 05 Jan. 2018].

[33] Alice.si. (2017). *Alice: Blockchain for good*. [online] Available at: http://alice.si/ [Accessed 05 Jan. 2018].

[34]Bernardo, P. (2017). *Cardano (ADA) Plans to Take Over the Eastern Pacific in 2018 – Price Prediction | Oracle Times*. [online] Oracletimes.com. Available at: https://oracletimes.com/cardano-ada-plans-to-take-over-the-eastern-pacific-in-2018-price-prediction/ [Accessed 15 Dec. 2017].

[35] Getmonero.org, The Monero Project. (2017). *Monero: Roadmap*. [online] Available at: https://getmonero.org/resources/roadmap/ [Accessed 15 Dec. 2017].

[36] Blockgeeks. (2017). *What is Bitcoin Cash? A Basic Beginners Guide - Blockgeeks*. [online] Available at: https://blockgeeks.com/guides/what-is-bitcoin-cash/ [Accessed 05 Nov. 2017].

[37] Bitcoincash.org. (2018). *Bitcoin Cash - Peer-to-Peer Electronic Cash*. [online] Available at: https://www.bitcoincash.org/ [Accessed 05 Nov. 2017].

[38] YouTube. (2015). *Pieter Wuille: Segregated witness and its impact on scalability*. [online] Available at: https://www.youtube.com/watch?v=NOYNZB5BCHM [Accessed 05 Nov. 2017].

[39] Blockgeeks. (2017). *What is Bitcoin Cash? A Basic Beginners Guide - Blockgeeks*. [online] Available at: https://blockgeeks.com/guides/what-is-bitcoin-cash/ [Accessed 05 Nov. 2017].

[40] CCN. (2018). *Bitmain Clarifies Its 'Bitcoin Cash' Fork Position*. [online] Available at: https://www.ccn.com/bitmain-clarifies-bitcoin-cash-fork-position/ [Accessed 11 Dec. 2017].

[41] CryptoCompare. (2017). *Bitcoin Cash / BCC (BCH) - Live Bitcoin Cash price and market cap*. [online] Available at: https://www.cryptocompare.com/coins/bch/overview/BTC [Accessed 05 Nov. 2017].

[42] Metz, C., Metz, C., Matsakis, L., Finley, K., Molteni, M., Matsakis, L., Harris, M. and Gregory, A. (2016). *The Biggest Crowdfunding Project Ever Was Supposed to Create Manager-free Companies. But It's a Mess*. [online] WIRED. Available at: https://www.wired.com/2016/06/biggest-crowdfunding-project-ever-dao-mess/ [Accessed 01 Nov. 2017].

[43] En.wikipedia.org. (2018). *IOTA (technology)*. [online] Available at: https://en.wikipedia.org/wiki/IOTA_(technology) [Accessed 18 Jan. 2018].

[44] Anon, (2018). [online] Available at: https://blockchain.info/charts/transactions-per-second?daysAverageString=7×pan=1year [Accessed 18 Jan. 2018].

[45] reddit. (2018). *how many transactions per second can IOTA process per second?* [online] Available at: https://www.reddit.com/r/Iota/comments/7dz3rq/how_many_transactions_per_second_can_iota_process/ [Accessed 18 Jan. 2018].

[46] Anon, (2018). [online] Available at: https://blockchain.info/pools [Accessed 18 Jan. 2018].

[47] En.bitcoin.it. (2017). *Category:History - Bitcoin Wiki*. [online] Available at: https://en.bitcoin.it/wiki/Category:History [Accessed 04 Jan. 2018].

[48] Tatar, J. and Burniske, C. (2017). *Cryptoassets*. McGraw-Hill Education, p.102.

[49]SEMrush. (2018). *Cryptocurrency study: search volume trends*. [online] Available at: https://d21buns5ku92am.cloudfront.net/46166/documents/34171-Cryptocurrencies%20study%20by%20SEMrush-405170.pdf [Accessed 03 Jan. 2018].

[50] Top Quality Articles & Tutorials. (2013). *Firefox 3 vs IE8 vs Google Chrome, Which Is the Winner?* [online] Available at: http://articles.pubarticles.com/firefox-3-vs-ie8-vs-google-chrome-which-is-the-winner-1279777582,28346.html [Accessed 03 Jan. 2018].

[51] Google.com. (2018). *How we started and where we are today | Google*. [online] Available at: https://www.google.com/intl/en/about/our-story/ [Accessed 03 Jan. 2018].

[52] Quandl.com. (2018). *Quandl*. [online] Available at: https://www.quandl.com/collections/markets/bitcoin-data [Accessed 18 Jan. 2018].

[53] Coinbase. (2018). *What countries are buys and sells available in?* [online] Available at: https://support.coinbase.com/customer/en/portal/articles/1392031-what-countries-are-buys-and-sells-available-in- [Accessed 25 Jan. 2018].

[54] En.wikipedia.org. (2017). *Mt. Gox*. [online] Available at: https://en.wikipedia.org/wiki/Mt._Gox [Accessed 03 Dec. 2017].

[55] YouTube. (2015). *Public & Private Keys Explained (Litecoin/Bitcoin)*. [online] Available at: https://www.youtube.com/watch?v=67uW07QDHxE [Accessed 02 Nov. 2017].

[56] Steemit.com. (2017). *Safely Claiming Bitcoin Fork Coins Like Bitcoin Cash* [online] Available at: https://steemit.com/bitcoin/@lukestokes/safely-claiming-bitcoin-fork-coins-like-bitcoin-cash [Accessed 05 Oct. 2017].

[57]Gov.uk. (2015). *HS284 Shares and Capital Gains Tax (2015) - GOV.UK*. [online] Available at: https://www.gov.uk/government/publications/shares-and-capital-gains-tax-hs284-self-assessment-helpsheet/hs-shares-and-capital-gains-tax-2015 [Accessed 05 Oct. 2017].

[58] Gov.uk. (2014). *Revenue and Customs Brief 9 (2014): Bitcoin and other cryptocurrencies - GOV.UK*. [online] Available at: https://www.gov.uk/government/publications/revenue-and-customs-brief-9-2014-bitcoin-and-other-cryptocurrencies/revenue-and-customs-brief-9-2014-bitcoin-and-other-cryptocurrencies [Accessed 05 Oct. 2017].

[59] Irs.gov. (2017). *Virtual Currency Taxes*. [online] Available at: https://www.irs.gov/pub/irs-drop/n-14-21.pdf [Accessed 25 Oct. 2017].

[60] LII / Legal Information Institute. (2017). *26 CFR 1.1012-1 - Basis of property.* [online] Available at: https://www.law.cornell.edu/cfr/text/26/1.1012-1 [Accessed 25 Oct. 2017].

[61] Cryptocompare.com. (2018). *CryptoCompare API - Cryptocurrency data API* [online] Available at: https://www.cryptocompare.com/api/ [Accessed 18 Jan. 2018].

[62] En.wikipedia.org. (2017). *John Bollinger*. [online] Available at: https://en.wikipedia.org/wiki/John_Bollinger [Accessed 16 Dec. 2017].

[63] Anon, 2017. J. Welles Wilder Jr. Wikipedia. Available at: https://en.wikipedia.org/wiki/J._Welles_Wilder_Jr. [Accessed 16 Dec. 2017].

[64] Cryptocompare.com. (2017) EOS (EOS) - Live EOS price and market cap. CryptoCompare. Available at: https://www.cryptocompare.com/coins/eos/charts/BTC?t=LC&p=6M [Accessed January 18, 2018].

[65] Bitfinex, (2017). *EOS Trading on Bitfinex*. Available at: https://www.bitfinex.com/posts/208 [Accessed January 18, 2018].

[66]Gokoluk, S., (2017). *To Win in Emerging Markets, Avoid the Passive Investing Rush. Bloomberg.com.* Available at: https://www.bloomberg.com/news/articles/2017-07-12/to-win-in-emerging-markets-avoid-the-passive-investing-rush [Accessed January 03, 2018].

27919466R00142

Printed in Great Britain
by Amazon